WITHOUT FEAR
OR FAVOUR

INTERPOL

Statement

"Northern Ireland has been the most dangerous place in the world to be a police officer. The risk factor in 1983 was twice as high as in El Salvador, the second most dangerous."

Many of the events that are retold here for the first time are among those that led Interpol to make that remarkable assertion.

A Shared Memoir

Of Some Who Crewed the Station Mobile Patrol Vehicle
'Bravo Delta Eight Zero.'

WITHOUT FEAR OR FAVOUR
Copyright © Andrew Martin, 2024

Paperback ISBN: 978-1-915223-38-8
All rights reserved.
Copyright Permission for Extracts from "Without Fear or Favour."

You are granted permission to reproduce and publish specific extracts from "Without Fear or Favour."

Unless authorised by the publisher, usage is restricted to ten percent of the total words in a story or up to three paragraphs. Any extracts must be accompanied by proper attribution to the book, author, and publisher. For any digital reproductions, it is required to include a hyperlink to the official website or a designated landing page for "Without Fear or Favour."

Every effort has been made to trace copyright holders and to obtain permission for the use of copyrighted material. The publisher apologies for any errors or omissions and would be grateful if notified of any corrections that should be incorporated in future reprints or editions of this book.

Due to ongoing threats, the names of individuals in this book have been changed.

The quotes used on the front and back cover of this book are from unknown sources.

Published by

Maurice Wylie Media
Inspirational & Christian Book Publisher

For more information visit: www.MauriceWylieMedia.com
Based in Northern Ireland, serving readers worldwide

Dedication

To the children of the officers who served in the Royal Ulster Constabulary; this book is dedicated to you.

May you always find strength in your mother's or father's legacy, pride in their service, and inspiration in their commitment to stand for what is right.

Contents

Foreword — 13

SECTION ONE

Introduction — 17
A Personal Testimony — 19
The La Mon Bomb Story and Its Legacy — 23
The Royal Ulster Constabulary — 31
    History — 31
    George Cross Awarded — 31
    Divisional Structure — 32
    Stations & Station Call Signs — 33
    Station Mobile Patrols & Call Signs — 34

Springfield Road RUC Station — 37
    History — 37
    'B' Division — 40
    Bravo Delta Subdivision — 41
    Bravo Alpha Subdivision — 41
    The Make-up of Vehicle Crews — 43
    On Duty Weapons — 44
    Personal Protection Weapons — 45

Springfield Road Station Party	45
The Hotspur Land Rovers	46
Postscript: A Genuine Surprise	49

SECTION TWO

My Personal Preamble to the Stories	53
Preface	55

STORIES

Chapter

1. 1st Radio Controlled Terrorist Booby Trap Bomb — 59
2. Members 1st Day of Duty in Bravo Delta Eight Zero — 67
3. John — 73
4. Attempt to Roll Bravo Delta Eight Zero — 77
5. Sniper Ambush at the Royal Victoria Hospital — 85
6. M60 Double Murder at Springfield Road Station — 91
7. Member Isolated on Foot in Hostile Area — 99
8. House Fire in Andersonstown — 109
9. An Encounter with and Assassin — 117
10. Watch The Person Beside You, He Could Be a Brit — 123
11. Bravo Delta Eight Zero High and Dry! — 129

12. Bravo Delta Eight Zero Stranded in Divis Complex!	133
13. IRA Terrorist Shot Dead Whilst on Active Service	141
14. Attempted Murder at RPG Avenue	147
15. The Ultimate Sacrifice	159
16. Plastics or Live Rounds	167
17. Contact, Contact at the 'Colins!'	175
18. Member Caught in Terrorist Blast Bomb Attack	179
19. First Hunger Striker to Break the Fast	185
20. Never, Ever, Forget Their Sacrifice	189
21. The Murder of an Artist	195
22. Heavy Gun Battle New Barnsley	199
23. Horizontal Mortar Bomb Attack, Falls Road	205
Statement	211
24. Attempt to Target Off-Duty Member	213
25. City Centre Ambush of Gerry Adams	217
26. No Creed in Duty, Paratrooper Sgt. Michael Willets	227
Epilogue	237
Contact	239

Foreword

For those who served with the Royal Ulster Constabulary in the late 1970s and 1980s, 'Without Fear or Favour' is an excellent book that provides the reader with a nostalgic step back in time.

One can experience the intensity, adrenaline, excitement, and fears that go with policing in many of the geographical areas in Northern Ireland where the Royal Ulster Constabulary was not accepted by some of the communities it served. Those who wore the uniform and policed the streets will revisit many of the emotions that came with the threat they faced day in and day out in the Division they policed or even at home.

This book provides community members who viewed the police officers in the grey Land Rover as faceless aggressors with the chance to look through the lens of the police officer. Police officers were real people with real feelings and, for the most part, wanted to serve the community they policed. Few attempts at recording the occurrences of those times presented the true face and feelings of the officers behind the armour.

For historians or those interested in the narratives of incidents and occurrences during the 'Troubles', this is an important memoir that can be used to offset or balance accounts from others. Police officers are reluctant to give their perspectives on events that occurred. There is no shortage of one-sided, undefended accounts of incidents that occurred that fall into the rhetoric and propaganda machines of the Republican agenda. This work goes some distance to balance the accounts for a few of those events.

Finally, to the families of those officers who fell during their service and to those who carry the physical and mental scars of what they went through, this is a record to show that you are not forgotten.

Dr. Philip Wright QPM
Retired Chief Superintendent RUC.

Section One

Introduction

The well-known phrase of 'Piggy in The Middle,' has as its definition in the Collins online dictionary this description, "Someone unwillingly involved in a dispute between two people or groups!" If ever there was a better description of the role which was thrust upon the Royal Ulster Constabulary throughout the period known as the Northern Ireland Troubles, we have yet to see it! So-called 'peacekeeping duties' between warring factions of Loyalists and Republicans, saw the force pilloried from both sides, in what very quickly became a totally 'no win' scenario.

Yet, that phrase does seem to carry a much more innocent connotation, perhaps one of children playing harmlessly in the safety of a school playground. But as we all know, there was nothing childlike, safe, or harmless about the role that the much battered and beleaguered police force faced on almost a daily basis.

Over the tumultuous years of conflict, many areas of our Province seemed to be particularly badly affected by the impact of the Troubles. Areas such as Belfast, Londonderry, and along the Border[1] are just a few among the many that will come to mind. Unquestionably residents from each of those areas would have their own harrowing tales to tell of those simply awful times. Sadly though, we do not doubt that the vast majority of the personal anecdotes from those areas, will for various reasons just be lost to the sands of time.

---

1 See The Border Cleansing, published in 2023 by Maurice Wylie Media under Truth Revealed Series.

Fearful that the stories which we have managed to gather together from old friends and colleagues, could similarly slip unseen into the dark recesses of history and consequently be lost forever, we firmly believe that this collective work of stories does merit being told.

It's an aspect of the Troubles narrative, that is rarely seen or heard, as the 'security implications' of daring to put your head above the parapet, even some 30 years into the peace process, could have serious consequences.

We have consciously tried to retell each story in what I hope is an easily understandable and straightforward manner. Each is recorded almost as a personal witness statement. Each of the narratives are verifiable as they relate to historical incidents, all of which occurred during a period of duty at Springfield Road.

A Personal Testimony

In 1973 as an energetic and enthusiastic 15-year-old school leaver, my life took a pathway which would have been very familiar to many young men in Northern Ireland back then, I started an apprenticeship. To be honest, from the day and hour I commenced that role, I kinda knew it wasn't for me. However, and mainly due to the fact that I didn't have a clue about what else I could do, and also because of a little pressure from my parents who believed and taught us that we should always try to finish what we start, I persevered. Consequently, some four years later I eventually qualified as a maintenance electrician.

My daily routine throughout those years, was that I would clock-in at 8 a.m. and clock-out at 5 p.m., with a half-hour lunch break from 12:30 p.m. to 1 p.m. Somehow or other, our half-hour lunch break often stretched to around forty minutes, and there was never an issue regarding that. Those additional few minutes were greatly appreciated, as they allowed me just enough time to nip home for a bite of lunch, and also call into a local newsagent where I would buy a daily newspaper. That daily purchase wasn't motivated by any academic interest in current affairs, no, the rationale behind this routine was for a much more basic reason. It was simply to enable me to keep up to date with all the news and gossip of 'The Beautiful Game,' football. Or to be even more specific, to keep abreast of any news of my beloved Manchester United.

Somewhat surprisingly then, it was actually headlines from the front-page of my daily newspaper which related to an incident that occurred on the evening of Friday, February 17, 1978, that was to grab my attention and help push my life in a direction that until then seemed highly unlikely!

The incident which I'm referring to, was of course the one which became known as the 'La Mon Massacre!' For those who are perhaps unaware of this incident, which was actually one of the worst atrocities throughout the duration of the Troubles, here is a brief summary.

That particular Friday evening, the La Mon Hotel, which to this day is located on the same site approximately ten miles outside Belfast, was the chosen location where members and friends of the Irish Collie Club were holding their annual dinner dance. Unbeknownst to them however, as they sat enjoying their dinner, members of an active service unit of the terrorist grouping the Irish Republican Army, were attaching a lethal incendiary bomb to the window of the very room which they were using.

I have copied and pasted below, a description which communicates far better than I could, the actual details of the bomb which the terrorists used that night.

'The bomb weighed about 45 pounds and had been placed within a leather hold-all. At its core was a detonator, a clothes peg which was used as a trigger, an alarm clock and finally a pound of home-made explosives. Packed around that core, were four one gallon-tin's which were each filled with petrol. The bomb had been specifically designed to throw the petrol out and ignite it instantaneously, thereby creating a huge fireball.'

In a recently published book by Rory Carroll entitled 'Killing Thatcher,' the author describes how the 'blast incendiary engulfed staff and guests at the La Mon Hotel,' that night. He goes on to describe the effect of the explosion, 'The device behaved like napalm, coating and scorching skin. Twelve people, all Protestants, were burned alive—one of the worst atrocities of the Troubles.'

Sometime in the aftermath of the incident, investigators recreated that bomb. Basing their re-construction on fragments and debris which had been recovered during the clear up at the scene, they tried to determine just how devastating the La Mon bomb explosion had been. From that mock-up explosion, they established that the resulting fireball was around 40 feet high and 60 feet wide. The force of the explosion blew shrapnel over the heads of the onlookers, who at that moment were standing some 400 yards away from the seat of the explosion!

The terrorist's bomb had literally been placed just a few feet from the largest concentration of diners, who were seated inside what was then known as the hotel's Peacock Room. It's believed that eight of the dead were sitting within about ten feet of the explosion and had been totally engulfed in the initial fireball.

Horrifically, at the inquests of those who perished, the state pathologist testified, 'They did not all die instantly!'

The La Mon Bomb Story and Its Legacy

The basic facts of this incident are really quite simple to explain, and indeed are adequately laid out in the preceding Personal Testimony paragraphs. However, articulating the full horror of what happened that night is much more difficult. I believe that it's only by looking beyond the facts and into the actual experiences of those who were there, that we can begin to grasp some semblance of the horror they went through.

To that end, the publisher of this book has included these very personal memories of La Mon survivors.

Tommy's story:

As a somewhat wayward and stubborn young teenager, I had not spoken to my parents for a couple of days, and indeed had we met in our home, there would have been no chatting between us. If pushed, they might have been lucky to get the odd grunt out of me!

Thankfully, that particular Friday night turned out a bit different, and to this day I still don't know why. Along with a couple of friends, we had spent the early hours of that evening wandering aimlessly round the streets of our local area. With nothing much happening, I decided that I would return home early, as I knew the snooker program 'Pot Black' was on the television, and that local favourite Alex Higgins was due to play Denis Taylor.

On arrival, I entered our kitchen, switched on the old black and white TV, and flopped into the big armchair to wait for the screen to give a picture.

It had just turned 8.30 p.m. and I could hear my parents upstairs busying themselves getting ready for their planned night out, at the nearby La Mon Hotel. They were in good spirits, and all 'done up' to go out. Dad had his suit on and Mum one of her favourite dresses and her hair all done nice. They really were the picture of happiness as they came into the kitchen before heading out to the car. They almost froze on the spot when they saw that I had returned home and that I was sitting watching the television. "Everything ok?" Mum asked, "Yeah," I grunted. I saw them shoot each other a glance as if to say we will just leave this and not push the conversation any further. Dad lifted the car keys and nodded to my mum, "Ready?" He asked her. Then it happened!

Don't ask me why, I can just about remember the words leaving my lips, "Are you not going to watch Pot Black before you go, it's Alex Higgins versus Denis Taylor?"

My parents were real TV snooker fans back then, and particularly keen on Higgy, but what had just happened was of much greater significance than that! I could almost hear their brains ticking over, as their faces betrayed the disbelief that their very uncommunicative teenage son had spoken to them and was inviting them to sit down with him! Not daring to push this situation, my Dad shrugged his shoulders toward my Mum, before taking off his jacket and putting it over the back of the chair. Mum, taking her cue (excuse the pun) from Dad, did the same before they both sat down to watch the match with me.

It wasn't a great match, Higgy wasn't in form, and a short while later, with the frame as good as finished, both stood up, replaced their jackets, and said "Right, we are off, if we do not see you later, we will see you in the morning," "aye, ok" was the grunted reply. I watched them get in the car and drive off to La Mon laughing and joking with each other.

It seemed to me that they had barely left, when I thought I heard what sounded like their car returning to our house. Unsure if I was just imagining this, I jumped up off my seat to have a look out the window to see what was happening. It was indeed my Dad's car drawing up again outside the house. Why on earth would they have returned home so quickly?

I noticed that after parking his car, Dad ran quickly round to Mum's side and opened the passenger door for her. Mum appeared to be in a real state, she was holding her head, and I could hear her crying, cries of anguish and pain. "Oh God no, no no no, please God help them!"

I asked, "What's happened, what's happened?"

My Mum was a really strong woman, she was the rock of our home, but at this point she was a quivering wreck, floods of tears were running down her face and she could barely stand or even talk, because of the level of her distress.

As they edged their way from the car into our home, Dad who was still supporting her, turned to me and said, "They've done La Mon, it's in flames." I knew who *they* were, it was the IRA.

We made our way into the living room, switching on the television to hear any breaking news stories. The rest of that night we spent trying to console each other, and wondering how many had died.

Over the years since, I often find myself inadvertently thinking back to the happenings in our family home that Friday night. It still amazes me how that one simple and seemingly inconsequential decision, to return home early and speak to my parents, had such a profound impact on all our lives. I'm so very conscious that things could so easily have turned out very different. I have absolutely no doubt that 'Pot Black,' Higgy, and Divine intervention gave me many more years with my parents, which I still thank the Lord for today.

My parents returned to La Mon many times after it was rebuilt. As for the night of the bombing it was seldom mentioned ever again, the pain was just too great. When they both died, I held their wakes at La Mon and though the service was as friendly as ever, those serving us never knew our history with the hotel or the part it played in our lives.

Survivor's personal story:

One of the married couples who were unfortunate enough to be in the Peacock Room at the Irish Collie Clubs Annual Dinner that night, were Billy and Lily McDowell. Both suffered horrific burn injuries, necessitating multiple skin grafts over many, many years. Despite suffering years of physical pain, it's the psychological impact of their experience that Billy refers to in this later statement, "It's not just the physical side of what took place that night, it is also the aftermath. For five years after it, Lily has been in and out of hospital having skin grafts done, she's had two or three nervous breakdowns, and these are things that people don't see or realise, even some of our own family will not realise it."

Lily McDowell graphically shared her memories of that night: "The bomb went off and it came like a ball of fire from the bottom of the room right up to the centre. It just looked like a huge orange ball.

I just crept away from the tables, not even knowing where to go as there was black smoke everywhere. The place was filled with smoke, and I knew I was going to die. I suddenly knew I had seconds. I sat up on my knees and as quickly as I could, I started to say my prayers. As I did so, and I know now, the presence of the Lord spoke to me. It was so still that I put my hands together and I was able to say 'The Lord's Prayer' from beginning to end without faltering at all.

After that, I just fell forward onto my face and I asked the Lord, "If it was in his will, that he would take me home as I was suffering so much, and let Billy live so he could look after my boys, my two boys." The next thing I remember I was being dragged by my foot and ankle through the door into the open air. I ended up with fifty percent third-degree burns and first-degree burns to my face and neck"

One severely burnt survivor described the inferno inside the restaurant as being "like a scene from hell," while another said the blast was "like the sun had exploded in front of my eyes."

Unsurprisingly in the immediate aftermath of the incendiary bomb explosion, the lights went out in the Hotel and thick, choking black smoke filled the room. The survivors, many with their hair and clothing on fire, rushed to escape the burning room. Total pandemonium ensued!

The first media reports regarding the bomb attack were broken by Downtown Radio, a short time later. This is their news report…

"Downtown Radio News, Ivan Little reporting. Reports are coming in of a bomb explosion in a hotel on the outskirts of Belfast. The bomb exploded at the La Mon House Hotel near Comber, a short time ago. First reports say there may be a number of casualties. Eye-witnesses said the explosion started a fierce fire which spread quickly through the building which was packed with hundreds of people attending dinner dances. It is understood a fleet of ambulances are on their way to the scene."

Consultant Anaesthetist Ronnie Armstrong was on duty at the Ulster Hospital in Dundonald that night, as the ambulances began to arrive with both the dead and injured on board.

Mr. Armstrong recalls: "Lying on the floor of the ambulance was what looked like three charred logs about four feet long and a couple of feet wide. At first, I did not register what they were. So, I went over and touched one and my finger went into it by one and a half inches deep and suddenly I hit something hard, it was then I realised this was a human being, but it was quite unrecognisable as such. I rapidly closed the ambulance door and went to enquire what the other two ambulances contained. I was given the understanding it was the same thing."

Alex Withers, who was one of the first firemen to arrive at the scene said, "I am satisfied that even if the fire appliances had been sitting in the carpark when the device went off, it would have been impossible to do anything for the people that were contained in the building. The only thing I could liken this to is Vietnam when a flamethrower or napalm would have been used."

It took firemen almost two hours to put out the blaze.

A retired RUC Detective Superintendent, the late Kevin Sheehy said, "This type of device had already been used by the IRA in more than one hundred attacks on commercial buildings before the La Mon attack. This was designed to stick to whatever it hit, a combination which caused severe burn injuries. A large number of these devices were produced by the IRA in 'bomb factories' in the Republic of Ireland."

The aftermath of the La Mon Hotel & Restaurant Firebomb.

The day after the explosion, from an office in Dublin, the following statement was released, "The IRA admits responsibility for the bombing operation at La Mon House, in which 12 innocent people died."

In the succeeding days, by way of mitigation, the republican propaganda machine repeatedly churned out reports to the effect that their members who had been involved in the planting of the bomb, had been frustrated in their efforts to phone in a suitable warning regarding it. They claimed that the actual phone which their members had tried to use was found to be 'Out of Order.' Consequently, they were unable to carry out that task on an appropriate time scale to allow the evacuation of the hotel.

Wesley Huddleston of La Mon Hotel Management said, "There was no warning relayed to us. When the police phoned the hotel to say there was a bomb at it, I told them it had already exploded.

It was as a direct response to this particularly horrific attack that I found myself personally challenged as to what part I was willing to play in helping the 'forces of law and order,' to combat the extremists in our country. Subsequently, I submitted my application form to join the Royal Ulster Constabulary, and by the following February (1979) I had commenced my initial training at the RUC Training Depot in Enniskillen.

As a consequence, it could be said, that my twenty-five-year police career partially came about, as a legacy of the La Mon bomb.

To help each reader get a fuller picture of what life was like as a police officer during these most turbulent times, I have included a very succinct description of the history of the RUC.

To a similar end, an overview of the forces operational structure, its practices and its procedures from back in the late 1970s and early 1980s is also recorded.

Above everything else though, this is just a simple collection of true and personal memories of dear friends and ex-colleagues.

"At the time we weren't aware that we were making memories, we were just too busy trying to stay alive!"

'The Depot, RUC Training Base, Enniskillen.' [2]

---

2   Copyright status is unknown.

The Royal Ulster Constabulary

History

Following partition and under the Government of Ireland Act of 1920, Northern Ireland with its Belfast-based government, became a distinct legal entity on May 3, 1921. Before this, the island of Ireland had of course been undivided and as one country had been under the governance of Britain. The Royal Irish Constabulary, which had been the country's existing police force since 1822, entered a phased process of disbandment on April 2, 1922. That process was completed on August 30 that same year.

This Act had seen the island of Ireland divided into two distinct countries, the Republic of Ireland and Northern Ireland, and also determined that two wholly new and distinct police forces would be established to police each of the newly formed states.

In Northern Ireland, the Royal Ulster Constabulary (RUC) was created and came into being on June 1, 1922. Records show that 1,330 members of the RIC joined the ranks of the RUC, whilst a mere 13 (thirteen) transferred to the Garda.

George Cross Awarded

On November 23, 1999, for its valiant stance against terrorism, Buckingham Palace announced that Her Majesty the Queen would award the George Cross to the RUC, in honour of its courage and dedication. Recognised as being the highest gallantry award in Britain, the George Cross is awarded solely, 'For acts of the greatest heroism or for most conspicuous courage in circumstances of extreme danger…'

The actual citation of the award reads:

> *"For the past 30 years the Royal Ulster Constabulary has been both the bulwark against, and the main target of, a sustained and brutal terrorist campaign.*
>
> *The force has suffered heavily in protecting both sides of the community from danger - 302 officers have been killed in the line of duty and thousands more injured, many seriously.*
>
> *Many officers have been ostracised by their own community and others have been forced to leave their homes in the face of threat to them or their families.*
>
> *As Northern Ireland reaches a turning point in its political development this award is made to recognise the collective courage and dedication to duty of all those who have served in the Royal Ulster Constabulary and who have accepted the danger and stress this has brought to them and to their families."*

Up until the RUC was ultimately subsumed into the Police Service of Northern Ireland on November 4, 2001, that force carried out its duties faithfully.

Divisional Structure

The deployment of its personnel and the structure of the RUC, was largely speaking, based around Northern Ireland's six geographic counties. With some minor alterations, more latterly to tie in with local

Council boundary changes, that remained the case throughout the history of the force.

Each defined area, was called a Division, and was nominally given an alphabetic name, ie. 'A' Division (Belfast City Centre area) right through the alphabet to 'P' Division (Ballymena area.) Each separate Division would have within its administrative structure, a Divisional Headquarters, a Sub-Divisional Headquarters, and then additionally a series of stations. It should be noted that the structure of Divisional boundaries, was for administrative purposes only. Every member of the force could serve throughout Northern Ireland.

The majority of the force's operational personnel, served within Divisions 'A' to 'F,' which broadly speaking covered the greater Belfast area. As previously mentioned, 'A' Division covered the main city centre shopping area. Then, loosely speaking, 'B' Division covered the West of the city, 'C' Division the Northwest, 'D' the North, 'E' the East and finally 'F' the South of Belfast.

Stations & Station Call Signs

Within this Divisional structure, each particular station was commonly named by its geographical location. For example, Andersonstown RUC Station covered the Andersonstown area of the city, and Oldpark RUC Station covered the Oldpark area, where each station was located.

Besides every station being given a name, each would additionally be assigned a radio call sign, consisting of two letters. All station call signs were determined by two identifying factors:

A/ Which police division the RUC Station was located in,
and,
B/ The actual name of the RUC Station.

To illustrate how this worked in practice, we will have a quick look at the two stations that I mentioned previously, Andersonstown and Oldpark. Andersonstown RUC, was a 'B' Division station, hence its call sign was prefixed with the call sign 'Bravo.' Obviously, the station name started with the letter 'A,' so the second identifying letter in its call sign would be 'Alpha.' Hence, Andersonstown RUC Station was identified as 'Bravo Alpha.'

Moving on then to Oldpark RUC Station, which was located in 'C' Division. Accordingly, it used the prefix 'Charlie,' followed by the first letter of the station name, 'Oscar.' Oldpark was accordingly identified as 'Charlie Oscar.'

This general practice was used for all the operational police stations throughout the Greater Belfast area. Rural areas differed.

However, there was one exception to this.

As I mentioned beforehand, each RUC Division had within its organisation a station which was identified as being the Divisional Headquarters Station. Each of those divisional Headquarters Stations, from 'A' Division right through to 'P' Division, was identified as 'Delta.' The divisional HQ of 'B' Division was Springfield Road, so it was known as 'Bravo Delta.' Tennent Street Station was the Divisional HQ for 'C' Division, hence its call sign was 'Charlie Delta,' and so on.

Station Mobile Patrols & Call Signs

Each operational station would generally have had one or more mobile patrol vehicles, operating within its designated geographical area. This patrol would be responsible for any 'calls' or 'incidents,' which required police attention throughout each particular period of duty.

The designation and call sign of each individual station, whether that be 'Bravo Delta,' 'Charlie Oscar' or whatever, was carried on through to that particular station's mobile patrols.

The general practice back in the day was that all Land Rover patrols carried the call sign 'Eight Zero, Eight One, Eight Two' etc. To illustrate just how this would have worked in practice, here is an example. A Land Rover patrol vehicle working out of Springfield Road, would have used the call sign, 'Bravo Delta Eight Zero.'

Saloon cars, whether armour-plated or not, used the call signs, 'Seven Zero, Seven One, Seven Two' etc. So, for example, a saloon car operating from Tennent Street in 'C' Division, would have been designated with the call sign 'Charlie Delta Seven Zero.'

Should any station have more than one patrol vehicle on operational duties, they would have simply kept the two-letter prefix but added to the number. I.e. The first patrol vehicle would be known as 'Eight Zero,' and any additional vehicles identified as 'Eight One, Eight Two' Etc.

Springfield Road RUC Station

Springfield Road RIC Station would later be the RUC Station
No 32 Springfield Road, Early 1900s

History

The actual RUC Station to which this work refers was in situ at 32 Springfield Road, Belfast from at least as far back as the early 1900's. However, there is evidence to indicate that there has been a police station on Springfield Road Belfast, as far back as 1886.

The Belfast Street Directory for 1901, records that address (32 Springfield Road) as being the Royal Irish Constabulary Barracks, and that it was under the authority of a Head Constable called John Magouran.

From an even earlier street directory, 1894, we discover that Springfield Road station was actually at a different location. Here it's recorded as being on the opposite side of the road and some four or five hundred yards further up the Springfield Road. It seems that the station back then was located at no. 10 Glenview Terrace, the last in a row of 10 large terrace houses just short of Cupar Street, and that a Sergeant O'Donnel was then in charge of the station party.

Since the station's relocation to 32 Springfield Road, it appears that the original building has gone through several extensive rebuilds. This has been particularly true from the late 1960's onwards, as over the succeeding years the stations fortifications were regularly improved, to help withstand the ever-growing threat of terrorist attacks.

No. 32 Springfield Road, RUC Station 1970's

Springfield Road RUC Station

No. 32 Springfield Road, RUC Station 1980's

The station's back gate from the outside, leading onto Cavendish Street

"DO NOT STAND AROUND IN THIS YARD"
Perhaps overstating the obvious!

'B' Division

'B' Division, during this particular period had five main operational RUC Stations, covering what was a densely populated, mostly working class, inner-city area. For administrative purposes this division was subdivided into two distinct areas, Springfield Road Subdivision and Andersonstown Subdivision. Included in the Springfield Road Subdivision were Hastings Street and New Barnsley. Andersonstown Station and Woodbourne Station made up the Andersonstown Subdivision.

Bravo Delta Subdivision: 3 Stations

1. Springfield Road. Divisional Headquarters

2. Hastings Street Station was located on Divis Street, between its junctions with Townsend Street and Millfield. This was right at the foot of the Falls Road, just before it merged into Castle Street.

3. New Barnsley Station was actually more of a Police post rather than a Police Station. Essentially it was a small temporary wooden structure, which sat within the larger and very heavily fortified army camp. It was located on the site of what was at one time known as The Henry Taggart Memorial Hall, which was on the upper part of the Springfield Road, just after Springfield Park.

Springfield Parade police post was yet another RUC base (of sorts) in the Springfield Road Sub-Division, which took on numerous roles over the years. However, during this particular period, it wasn't an operational Police Station.

Bravo Alpha Subdivision: 2 Stations

1. Andersonstown Station, the Subdivisional Headquarters, was to be found at the road junction where the Falls Road meets both the Glen and the Andersonstown Roads. History records that as far back as 1905, the Andersonstown barracks was located here. Indeed, quite remarkably at one time it is reported that the station party consisted of only 2 men! Imagine!

2. Woodbourne Station, which is located quite a bit further out on the Stewartstown Road, is a relatively newly built station. Prior to being redeveloped as a police barracks, it was initially a large family home. From that purpose it was converted for use as a hotel. Trading under the name of The Woodbourne Hotel, it became a very popular wedding venue.

Unfortunately, with the huge shifts in population which occurred during the early years of the Troubles, it soon became isolated on what had become a community interface. Soon after it became the target for terrorist bombs, and around 1970 it was destroyed.

In addition to the Police stations listed above, during this period there were numerous Army bases located throughout the Division, North Howard Street, MaCrory Park for example. It was normal practice back then to have a number of Police officers stationed at each of those military bases.

Without wanting to state the obvious, Springfield Road RUC Station, like all the others within B Division, was fully operational 24 hours a day, 365 days a year. The actual station manpower would have fluctuated considerably over the years, depending on numerous factors. However, given that most of the incidents recorded in this work refer to the period of the late 1970's through to the early 1980's, from personal memory I will try to throw some light on the makeup and indeed the actual numbers of the station manpower around that time.

It should be borne in mind however, that matters such as staffing levels and shift patterns, changed on a fairly regular basis due to the operational requirements of the time. Normally speaking, each 24-hour period would have been policed by three different sections of police, A section, B section and C section. A fourth section, D, would at this time be off duty, on rest days.

The actual hours worked to cover the full 24-hour period, would have included three eight-hour shifts. The shift pattern back then, was 7-3 (early) 3-11 (late) and 11-7 (night.) Each of the four sections would have been made up of around 10-12 Constables, 1-2 Sergeants and 1 Inspector. Where possible, each of these sections would have had a Policewoman included in its number, for those duties which would specifically require a female officer.

Before any 'real operational police work' could take place, additional daily responsibilities would regularly have seen each section's numbers dramatically reduced. Particularly true on the 'early' shift, members routinely found themselves detailed for 'out-duties.' These included tasks such as Crown Court Duties, Court Appearances, Security Duties, Football and Public Order Duties. Force Training, Public Order Training and things like Annual Leave, Sick Leave and even Sports Leave, meant that it was only on very rare occasions that any section would ever report for duty, with a full quota.

The Make-up of Vehicle Crews

As I have tried putting this collective work together, into what I hope is both a readable and accurate reflection on the particular incidents listed, I have quite unconsciously found myself defaulting to what could be referred to as 'Police Speak.' By this I mean using particular words and phrases, which at one time were common within police circles. So, to help those who are perhaps unfamiliar with terms such as 'observer,' or 'extra observer,' et.al., I'll take a few minutes to explain the meaning and significance of these terms.

Each of Springfield Road's four operational 'shifts,' would at all times have tried to maximise their vehicular patrol capacity. Get as many patrols as possible on the streets. However, it must also be pointed out, that aim would never have been at the cost of endangering its members.

For a section to put a patrol vehicle on the road, they would have required a bare minimum of three members. The composition of a vehicle crew which would have been detailed at a pre-duty briefing by the section's Sergeant or Inspector, would have included a driver, an observer and at least one extra observer.

The driver's role in the crew requires no explanation; however, the role of the others mightn't be just so obvious.

The observer, who would have had the front passenger seat of the vehicle designated to him/her, would also have been the member of the crew who would have been accountable for any and all calls during that particular period of duty. The observer's accepted 'right' to the front passenger seat, held true with one exception. Should the patrol at any stage have been joined by a senior officer, whether that be a Sergeant, Inspector or whatever, with respect to that rank the observer would then have succeeded his seat, whilst he in turn would have moved into the rear of the vehicle.

The role of the extra observer, whether there were one, two or three of them, would have included providing additional armed support for the observer and the patrol vehicle throughout the duration of the shift. Consequently, in addition to their own personal protection weapon, they would have routinely carried an additional firearm. A weapon, such as an M1 Carbine or a Sterling Machine Gun would have been issued from the station armoury for this purpose. This gun would have been returned to the armoury at the end of each shift.

On Duty Weapons

M1 Rifle

Sterling Machine Gun

Personal Protection Weapons

Walther PPK
Up until late 1979

Ruger Revolver Speed Six
Post 1979

Springfield Road Station Party

The Springfield Road RUC Station party also included a Station Sergeant, a Station Inspector, a Chief Inspector, a Superintendent and the Divisional Commander, who was a Chief Superintendent.

In addition to those roles listed above, working behind the scenes there would also have been additional police personnel who were responsible for other more routine duties. These included responsibilities such as Warrants, Uniforms, Transport, Stores and several administrative roles. In total, perhaps an additional 6-8 constables.

In the early 1980s, Springfield Road saw its first appointments of unarmed Civil Servants, who were assigned various roles to assist Police with what was termed as administrative or non-operational duties. Supposedly, this additional manpower would allow our authorities to free up any police personnel, who had been tied up performing administrative roles to that point.

The Hotspur Land Rover

Before moving on to the personal stories which are of course the essence of this book, it would be remiss of me not to give a mention to the actual Land Rover patrol vehicles.

Honestly, it would be hard to imagine just how the RUC would ever have coped without access to the tried and tested Land Rover vehicles. First adapted and used by the RUC in 1957, I believe that in this instance it's fair to make use of what has become a very overused expression in Northern Ireland politics; the RUC and the Land Rover are indeed truly inextricably linked! To the extent that books have been written regarding this very topic.

However, without exploring this subject too deeply, I will try to give a synopsis of the development of the Land Rover, and its value to those who used it daily in Springfield Road during this period.

Initially the Land Rover's which were used by the RUC in Northern Ireland, were what would have been referred to as 'Soft Skins.' The name says it all!

An Early Soft Skin Land Rover
Note the Makrolon Outer Skin

Those early vehicles, whilst able to withstand stone and bottle attacks, had no armour which was able to protect their passengers from gunfire! Consequently, it became obvious that in many areas throughout the Province, driving about in 'soft skin' vehicles was just too dangerous. To do their job in certain shall we say, sensitive areas, police required a vehicle which could withstand gunfire.

To this end, the 1st generation 'Hotspur' was developed. Taking its name from the Welsh armoured steel manufacturing company which provided the necessary materials, and by using their own engineers and mechanics to put the vehicles together, the RUC were now in possession of a vehicle which was custom-built for the job!

Over the succeeding years, the Hotspur armoured Land Rover proved itself indispensable! As each year of the Troubles passed into the history books, increasing numbers of grateful Police Officers could testify to the protective role played by the Hotspur Land Rover.

The 'boffins' in the Police workshops continued developing the security features of the Hotspur, always trying to remain one step ahead of the ever-increasing deviousness of the terrorists.

A later version of a RUC Hotspur with Protective Front & Side Skirts

An RUC Hotspur Land Rover without Protective Front & Side Skirts

Postscript: A Genuine Surprise!

Embarking on a work of this kind, which has by its very nature entailed meeting up with old colleagues and reminiscing about stories in which we each played a part, isn't exactly a prime recipe for surprises or shocks. Or so I thought!

However, whilst researching the history and locations of Springfield Road Station, I came across a story that has both surprised and shocked me!

On Friday April 10, 1970, both of Northern Ireland's main daily newspapers, The Belfast Telegraph and The News Letter, each reported that on the previous day, the Royal Ulster Constabulary had opened a new police station at number 669 Springfield Road. The premises chosen to house this new station was nothing grander than a vacant end terrace house, (one of three) which overlooked the main Springfield Road and was situated in the New Barnsley housing development.

It seems that over the previous weeks, there had been numerous unsavoury clashes between sections of the local community and the Army, who by then had a base in the locality. The Henry Taggart Memorial Hall, (About 200 metres further down Springfield Road.)

The plan was that this new Police station, which was to be manned 24 hours a day, would offer the local community a 'better point of contact.' To this end the new station would be manned by an experienced Station Sergeant and he would be assigned a full complement of Constables. They would of course still have the continued assistance and supportive presence of RUC mobile patrols which worked out of the main Springfield Road barracks.

Initially at least, these additional police presence seemed to be well received by the local community, as the newspapers report that the station was busy with a stream of callers throughout the day. A spokesman for the police is recorded as saying, "The signs are that people need the station. Things are going extremely well and quite a number of calls have already been handled."

However, and perhaps unsurprisingly, given the unprecedented levels of community tension and open street conflict that had engulfed the area, attitudes towards the police quickly changed. Consequently, after what had been a determined and committed three-hour onslaught which took place from around 3:30 p.m. on the afternoon of Saturday June 27, the new station was to be completely overrun and then ransacked by gangs of marauding Republican rioters.

Four police officers, who at that time would have been unarmed as per the recommendations of the 1969 Hunt Report, were caught inside the station. Having been totally surrounded and besieged by the rioters, eventually made their way to safety when a unit of armed military personnel came to their rescue.

The station at 669 Springfield Road, which was located to be 'a better point of contact for the local community,' lasted from Thursday April 9, until Saturday June 27. A total of just over 11 weeks. Needless to say, it was never reopened.

Section Two

My Personal Preamble To The Stories

From 1979 and for almost 25 years thereafter, I was an immensely proud member of the Royal Ulster Constabulary. Like many of my colleagues who were also recruited and served over that particular period, I had joined the Force conscious of the need and was willing to stand in the frontline of the ongoing war against terrorism. The 1970s was a particularly intense and traumatic period of the 'Troubles,' with an ever-present threat to every member who put on that bottle green uniform.

It now seems extraordinarily demoralising that even after 30 years of the 'Northern Ireland Peace Process,' we still live our lives under what is a tangible threat from active dissident republicans! Whether that threat is as real as we believe, hardly seems to matter as many of us continue to perform those well-drilled-in extra security routines, that kept us alive throughout those dark days. Some of which will be shared within this book.

A large number of today's mental health professionals would define the diagnosis of post-traumatic stress disorder (PTSD), as being a normal human reaction to an abnormal situation. Considering the disturbing and abnormal nature of many of the occurrences that lie behind their stories, it's hardly surprising that so many of these extraordinarily brave ex-police officers now display symptoms of that particular mental health condition.

Having had the privilege to have served in Springfield Road RUC Station for three momentous years, from 1979 to 1982, I have long felt that these stories warrant retelling. Especially when the narrative of the

'Northern Ireland Troubles' has been written and rewritten to suit the political climate of the day, and even to this day remains in a state of flux. The views and stories of both Loyalists and Republican paramilitaries have been well represented in any narrative that I have ever come across. Yet by comparison, the voice, and the stories of those who were tasked to 'Keep the Peace' throughout that period, remains almost silent.

Preface

A note on how I have chosen to record and present each of these individual stories.

One of the most basic principles of English Law asserts that in any legal case, the onus is exclusively on 'the person who makes the allegation, to prove the case.' In simple terms this means that the burden of proof regarding any alleged offence or crime, lies totally with the person who makes the allegation! Further, there is no such 'onus' on a so-called defendant to prove their innocence!

Subsequently, from the earliest days of our initial training in Enniskillen, recruits were taught the importance of gathering evidence and then shown how to record witness statements in a manner which would be acceptable in a court of law. The importance of recording such statements in this way, really cannot be overstated.

In the first instance, even before recording what any witness has to say, it is important to establish their bona-fide and legitimacy. This would generally be asserted at the earliest possible opportunity. Only after validating the credibility of the witness, would we then move on to recording their statement.

The actual statement should, where possible, be written in the witness's own words and recorded in the first person. By this we mean that we would only record what that particular witness either saw, heard or felt. Hence it would be written down as 'I saw, I heard, or I felt!'

It's also worth mentioning what cannot be included in a statement of evidence, witnesses cannot testify to what someone else saw or heard or felt.

Such statements would be recorded on an official RUC witness statement pro-forma, a form called 38/36.

As a consequence, after spending time with my colleagues and listening to their accounts, when it came to putting them in writing for this work, I simply reverted to type!

Not only was this the most natural way for me to re-tell these hard-hitting stories, I believe it also makes them much more authentic and readable. Each story is therefore preceded with a very brief couple of sentences, showing its context.

Some forty odd years later, they remain emotive and very difficult to talk about for many of those involved.

Stories

CHAPTER 1

1st Radio Controlled Terrorist Booby Trap Bomb

Diary Date:	December 19, 1978.
Incident:	1st Radio Controlled Terrorist Booby Trap Bomb in Belfast.
Background:	Normal Early Shift Springfield Road.
Storyteller:	Brian.

On December 19, 1979, the News Letter[3] published an article (see next page) that carried the headline, *'Bomb victim fought back from the shadow of the grave.'* As I'm sure many of you who are reading this will no doubt be aware, inevitably behind headlines of that particular nature, lie life stories of great heartache and much suffering.

Sadly, this story is no different.

---

3 The News Letter is one of Northern Ireland's main daily newspapers. It is the world's oldest English-language general daily newspaper still in publication, having first been printed in 1737.

> # Bomb victim fought back from shadow of the grave

Newspaper Headline December 19, 1979.

A full year before the publication of that particular headline, the harrowing event that precipitated it, occurred in Forfar Street, Belfast. On what the police believed to be yet another 'errand of mercy,' they again became the unsuspecting victims of an evil terrorist plan.

Here's the story.

On the morning of Tuesday, December 19, 1978, I reported for the early 7 a.m. – 3 p.m. shift with my colleagues. At our pre-duty briefing, I was detailed as an extra observer in the main station mobile patrol. Our crew that day was made up of a further two Constables, one of whom was driving, and we were also joined by our section Sergeant.

Whilst on general patrol in the Springfield Road area around 9 a.m., or perhaps slightly earlier, we were made aware that a report had come in to police of a suspicious car sitting in the Forfar Street area, and that it had been sitting there overnight. We made our way to Forfar Street travelling via Springfield Drive, which back then ran from the main Springfield Road down to Forfar Street just opposite the front gates of James Mackie & Sons engineering company.

Springfield Drive, looking down from the main Springfield Road to the front gates of Mackie's. Forfar Street runs Left to Right, just in front of the Gates.

When we arrived at the junction of Springfield Drive and Forfar Street, we could see the car which had been reported as suspicious. It was parked fairly close to this junction, immediately to our left, and on the opposite side of the street to the long red-brick wall, which at that time flanked the Mackies factory. There was enough room between the Springfield Drive junction, and the precise location of the suspect car on Forfar Street, to allow our driver to pull in and stop at what we felt was a safe enough distance away.

When I clambered down and out of the back of our vehicle, I remember walking towards the car. Indeed, I remember walking right past it before stopping and looking around for somewhere that I could kneel down to take 'cover.' At this stage I noticed that my Sergeant was approaching the suspect vehicle on foot. I can't be 100% certain on this, but I'm nearly sure that I actually walked past the vehicle on what would have been its passenger's side, whilst my Sergeant's approach definitely took him to the driver's side.

What happened next, even though it was over 40 years ago, still seems absolutely surreal to me! It was almost dreamlike or perhaps even illusory! It's honestly such a difficult experience to put into words or describe adequately. But the next thing I remember was seeing a huge flash of light! It almost seemed that I had been engulfed in a sheet of lightning! That was followed, almost in an instant, by a deafeningly loud boom. Simultaneously, I was lifted off my feet and propelled down the street, by an invisible energy or force! I landed on my back, but seemingly uninjured I was able to jump back up immediately and make my way back over to what was by then a scene of devastation!

My Sergeant, who literally could have been no more than three or four feet from the explosion, had taken the full force of the blast. It seemed that he was on fire and was in a real bad way. As my other colleagues went to his assistance, I ran across to our vehicle where I tried to radio in a report of the incident and ask for immediate help! I remember the radio controller replying to me to the effect that I should calm down, and slowly repeat the message! I was running on pure adrenaline and just couldn't seem to control my speech! I do recall hearing another call-sign, possibly Bravo Delta Eight One, reporting that they were en-route to assist us and weren't that far away. The controller re-emphasised to them that on their arrival at the scene, they should give him a better situation report than what I had been able to up to that point.

I seem to remember that workers from the nearby Mackies factory, who must have heard the explosion, were very quickly on the scene. They provided much-needed help and basic first aid, until the emergency services arrived at the scene. On their arrival they immediately attended to those who were injured, then transported the casualties to the nearby Royal Victoria Hospital for medical treatment.

Postscript

Of the four-man RUC Land Rover crew who attended the report of a suspicious vehicle in Forfar Street that day, miraculously, three walked away almost unscathed. But as proclaimed in that shocking 1979 News Letter headline, 'Bomb victim fought back from the shadow of the grave,' that was far from the case for the RUC Sergeant who was the fourth member of that day's crew of Bravo Delta Eight Zero.

Sergeant Noel McConkey was the officer in charge of the Springfield Road Land Rover patrol that morning, and it was he who took the brunt of the terrorist's devious radio-controlled booby trap bomb.

For the newspaper article which accompanied that startling headline in the News Letter back in 1979, Noel gave a fairly substantial and indeed graphic retelling of his memories of that day's horrific event. To finish this account of that morning's story and with his permission, I have drawn heavily on that particular interview. I have also had access to other newspaper accounts which relate to the events of that Tuesday morning in December 1978.

The first paragraph of that 1979 article, is very graphic and leaves little to the imagination.

'Noel McConkey lost both legs and an arm, in a 50lb car bomb blast a year ago today - but has confounded medical experts by being alive to tell the tale.'

In essence, that 30-word paragraph tells the fundamentals of both that day's events, and also the anguish of the following year. But to leave this story at that point, would I believe do Noel and indeed all those who suffered at the behest of terrorists, yet another injustice. I feel that it's only by revealing the detailed choreography that led up to that day's bomb, that perhaps people will begin to grasp the magnitude of the evil that stalked our country in those days!

Noel in particular, but also of course those colleagues who were with him that morning, had the awful misfortune of being the very first members of the security forces within the Greater Belfast area to suffer the devilish consequences of the IRA's latest invention, the radio-controlled car bomb.

The upshot of this new development was far-reaching, giving terrorists even more control of their planned bombing atrocities! They could quite literally plant their device, retreat to a safe point where they could observe the ongoing activity around that area, then at what would seem to them as the optimal time, simply flick a switch, and then Boom! I have no doubt, to a greater or lesser extent, that is exactly what happened in Forfar Street that fateful morning.

However, without firsthand knowledge from those who perpetrated this attempt to murder police, it's difficult to be precise or dogmatic about just how their plans unfolded. Having said that, I would 'guess' that that day's particular sequence of events would have followed this pattern.

Sometime beforehand they would have 'acquired' a suitable car, before driving it to what would have been a secure location. Once there, and without time constraints, they would carefully have setup and secreted the bomb within the vehicle, with a very simple radio receiver attached. When the vehicle was fully prepared and ready to go, perhaps even under the cover of darkness, the terrorists would then have taken it to their chosen location, Forfar Street.

The preparation for this particular bomb-attack, undoubtedly would also have included finding a 'friendly' house in that Forfar Street area. Ideally, the house selected would give the bombers a good vantage point, overlooking the location where they planned to leave their booby-trapped car.

Then, with the car now safely in position, perhaps three or four armed terrorists would have moved into the house to carry out the attack. Conceivably they would then have waited for a genuinely unsuspecting local resident to report the presence of a non-local or suspicious vehicle to the police. Or indeed, they might even have done that themselves! Then, without even having to step out from the security of the house in which they were held-up, they had the simple task of waiting for the police to arrive before triggering the bomb at their chosen time.

It seems that the terrorist bomber did indeed wait for what he considered to be the 'optimal' moment to explode the device. The terrorist appears to have watched and waited as the first police officer, Brian, walked past the car on its passenger side. Then, as Noel was approaching the car on the offside, the side in which they had placed the device, they triggered the bomb!

When back-up, in the shape of additional police and military arrived they were faced with a truly sickening scene! Noel's three colleagues were what would be termed as 'walking wounded,' but his particular situation was horrific. In that News Letter article of 1979, part of his personal reminiscence of the actual incident includes this paragraph, which I've adjusted slightly to help contextualise it.

> *"Not realising the severity of my injuries, I tried to get up.*
> *I remember the ambulance man saying to me in a comforting voice,*
> *'It's all right son, we'll lift you.'*
> *It didn't occur to me at the time, that I was actually eased onto a*
> *blanket instead of a stretcher, because my body was so mutilated!"*

The ambulance medics did all they could to stabilise Noel's condition, before transferring him to the nearby Royal Victoria Hospital. Such was his injuries and due to the amount of blood loss he suffered, the stark reality was that if the incident had occurred any further away from the hospital, Noel simply wouldn't have survived. His immediate plight was further complicated due to having a particularly rare blood group, which meant that supplies had to be flown into the Royal from all over the province. Military helicopters were deployed for this purpose, and in total 56 pints of blood was required to save his life.

Eventually though, having endured eight major operations and to the surprise of many, a full five months after he was first admitted, Noel was transferred from the Royal Victoria Hospital to Musgrave Park Hospital. There, his recovery continued, and he commenced the rehabilitation work which would eventually see him able to return home to his family, whose love and support had never wavered throughout these most difficult of times.

CHAPTER 2

Members 1ˢᵗ Day of Duty in Bravo Delta Eight Zero

Diary Date:	June 4, 1979.
Incident:	First Day of Duty in Bravo Delta Eight Zero.
Background:	Normal Late Shift Springfield Road.
Storyteller:	Andrew.

Having entered the RUC Depot in Enniskillen on February 25, 1979, as part of 'Y' Squad, our group eventually 'Passed Out' on May 16. Incidentally, my starting date was just about one year and one week after the La Mon bombing, which had played such a part in pushing me in this direction.

After leaving the Depot, I, like all other recruits, had been informed only of the Police Division which I would be assigned to, and not of the particular station within that division. It would be several weeks later, during additional training, before I learned which station that would be.

As part of RUC post depot training, recruits underwent Firearms Training. This was conducted in a set of dilapidated buildings in East Belfast, at the Connswater Police post. While attending the training there, I was informed that I would be posted to Springfield Road Station and assigned to 'D' Section. I distinctly remember mentioning to my colleagues over tea in the Connswater canteen, that I had absolutely no idea where Springfield Road Station was located. Before joining the police, I had only been to Belfast around a dozen times - a surprising fact by today's standards. I vividly recall one of my colleagues sarcastically suggesting that if I ever got lost, I could simply find the back entrance of Belfast City Hall and then walk straight out of the city in a rural direction to locate the police station. Very simple advice, but to his credit, he was correct.

On Wednesday, June 4, I reported for my first official day's duty as an RUC Constable. At some point over the intervening time, I had been informed that due to the security situation, Springfield Road police personnel were not permitted to drive directly into the station. Instead, they were required to report to Hastings Street station, which was deemed to be a safer location to drive into. From there, transport would be provided up to Springfield Road in the back of an Army Humber Saracen - a vehicle affectionately known as a 'Pig'. This arrangement would eventually change to a different location in the coming years.

An Army 'Pig' Just After Leaving Springfield Road RUC Station.

That day our section was scheduled to be on the late shift, which ran from 3 p.m. to 11 p.m. So, to allow time for onward transport from what in essence was a staging area, Hastings Street, we reported to that location for 2:30 p.m. Now, despite having completed all my training and being deemed (by my authorities) ready to face the 'mean streets of Belfast,' I honestly can't remember ever feeling so unprepared and out of my depth. I was well outside my comfort zone!

On arrival at Hastings Street, we parked our cars and waited for the appearance of our transport. With its military driver and another colleague acting as his escort, (riding shotgun,) the Pig eventually trundled noisily into the Hastings Street yard. That afternoon there were 9 or 10 of us waiting for the lift, and we dutifully piled into the back before it struck out for what was a very uncomfortable 10–15-minute drive up and into the station yard at Springfield Road. Just as soon as the Pig stopped, we debussed and made our way into the station. We then set about getting ready for our turn of duty. Meanwhile, the army Pig just sat there waiting for the early crew to finish their shift, before transporting them back down to Hastings Street.

I think it's important to mention what was a really convoluted transport issue which members of Springfield Road faced on a daily basis. When the prearranged lifts ran smoothly, with everyone reaching the pick-up point on time, it was a workable situation. However, if for a myriad of genuine reasons, you happened to miss the shift pick-up, your transport to Springfield Road station then became a tortuous game of hit and miss. If you were lucky, a passing police or military vehicle could pick you up, and you could be in Springfield very quickly. However, if your timing was bad and all operational vehicles were either tied up or busy, you could be left twiddling your thumbs at Hastings Street for hours!

On reflection, I would have to say that Springfield Road was a truly wonderful station to have served in. However, there were occasions when the whole experience seemed quite surreal, which the bizarre transport arrangements only added to.

Back to my first day's duty at Springfield Road. During the crew briefing, I was detailed by my section sergeant to act as an extra observer in the station mobile patrol, Bravo Delta Eight Zero. The standard operational procedure for an extra observer at that time, required that I sign a Sterling machine gun plus two full magazines of ammunition (30 rounds) out of the station armoury, and subsequently provide armed cover for the vehicle during that period of duty.

Sterling Submachine Gun
(SMG)

Unsurprisingly, that evening passed by in a blur, but I do remember that the crew made every effort to make sure that I felt welcome. They tried to show me around as much of our 'patch' as possible, and the night appeared to be going well. Then, just as the light began to fade, our driver, who also happened to be the senior man of our section, mentioned that he would take us down to the Lower Falls area for a quick drive through the Divis Flats complex. I seem to remember that he, or perhaps one of the other crew members, mentioned that it would be good for me to have a quick look around that particular area! Honestly, he did!

On arrival at Divis, I noticed a large crowd of youths hanging around what seemed to be a small fire on some waste ground at the bottom of the main Divis Tower building. Our driver mounted the curb and cautiously drove the Land Rover toward the crowd. However, when we came to a stop fairly close to the small fire, most of those hanging about seemed to have disappeared into the flats complex. Both our driver and front seat observer then got out of the vehicle, and the other extra observer who was in the back of the vehicle with me, said we should also dismount to provide armed cover for our colleagues. He continued, mentioning that while he was about to move forward to a cover point nearer to where the driver and the observer were standing, he suggested that I remain at the side of our Land Rover. Once out of the vehicle, I noticed that our driver and observer were both over-talking to the youths at the fire. I did exactly what I was told, holding as tightly as humanly possible to the side of the armoured Land Rover.

Almost inevitably, the conversation between the gang of youths and my colleagues seemed to get heated. As they then made their way back towards the vehicle, some stones and a couple of bottles were thrown in our direction. The mood of the situation had changed in an instant. The crowd, which by then had regrouped, seemed increasingly agitated and was edging their way closer and closer to our vehicle. Just as the other crew members had returned to the vehicle and before I had moved my position to climb into the back, I was startled beyond belief when I heard an almighty thud of something striking the side of our vehicle, right beside my head! When I looked around to see what had happened, I noticed that lying on the ground, no more than two feet from where I was standing, was a small wooden shafted hatchet! Within the space of 30 seconds, what had seemed to have been a relatively peaceful, if not friendly, encounter between the police and some local youths had turned into a situation that, for our safety, we had to make a speedy withdrawal from.

As I mentioned, this incident took place just as darkness was falling, indicating that our shift was coming to an end. And despite my remarkably close encounter with some of the not-so-friendly locals, I had otherwise survived unscathed! Back at the station and on terminating our days duty, rather than just jumping into the army shuttle, and heading home, several of our crew headed upstairs to the military Sergeant's Mess. It was located on the third floor of the station building and doubled up as a small bar. (Perhaps to be kind I should use the term intimate!) There, we were able to sit down and relax over a couple of quiet pints. We spent an hour or so just chatting about how the day had gone.

Considering that this was all of 45 years ago, unbelievably, a couple of things remain vivid in my memory regarding that visit to the Mess. The first thing was the price of the beer! Somehow or other we were able to buy four pints for the princely sum of one pound! Yes, 1 'Quid' for 4 Pints! Unbelievable!

The second thing that I recall, was that whilst chatting over how my very first turn of duty had gone, I happened to mention to those sitting around the table, that perhaps they hadn't noticed, but that I very nearly had my head chopped off by a hatchet! Cue much sarcastic laughter, followed by a big swallow of beer, before one of my colleagues in a very official and extremely mockingly authoritative voice replied, "And welcome to 'D' Section Springfield Road young fella!"

CHAPTER 3

John

Diary Date:	Spring/Summer 1979.
Incident:	A Long Lonely Walk.
Background:	No Transport Available.
Storyteller:	Andrew.

In the previous chapter I mentioned some of the difficulties which faced serving officers due to being unable to drive directly into their home station, Springfield Road.

To help illustrate just how problematic this situation was, here's a somewhat humorous story, which to be honest I had forgotten about, but was reminded of whilst reminiscing with another ex-colleague.

John, who sadly is no longer with us, was a much valued and trusted colleague to everyone he served with. He was what some might call a 'battle-hardened,' trustworthy senior Constable, who could always be relied on for some sage words in any situation.

At the time of this incident, or should I say this adventure, John was working out of Springfield Road Station, but he was on detachment duty as an Army Liaison officer at Macrory Park Army Base on the Whiterock Road. Or, in very simple terms, he was temporarily attached to the military battalion in Macrory, and his daily duty would have seen him accompany the Army on foot patrols throughout the surrounding areas. Macrory Park was a very isolated and dangerous location for members of the security forces. It was totally surrounded by hostile neighbourhoods, such as Britton's Parade, Westrock, Whiterock, The Rocks and the Falls Road.

On what was a lovely bright spring Saturday morning in 1980, John had started work early and had been out on an extended foot patrol with his Army colleagues, in and around the local area. On their safe return to Macrory Park, John, as per normal practice reported this to the police radio control room at Springfield Road.

He went on to ask if the controller, (Call sign Bravo Delta,) would arrange to have an RUC Land Rover pick him up at Macrory Park, (Call sign Bravo Mike) and transport him down to Springfield Road for an important prearranged appointment. The controller acknowledged this request but explained that at that moment all the station vehicles were busy, and it could be some time before his requested transport would occur.

Over the next half hour or so, John's increasingly angst voice could be heard on the divisional radio repeatedly asking,

"Bravo Delta, Bravo Delta from Bravo Mike. Further to my earlier requests, are there any vehicles free yet, as I really need to get to your location for my appointment."

With the best will in the world and despite Johns repeated earnest requests, there were simply no vehicles available, and it just seemed that on this occasion he would have to miss his appointment. However, John being John, was nothing if not resourceful. And perhaps even a wee bit eccentric!

Having eventually come to the realisation that the lift he had been looking for, simply wasn't going to materialise, he decided that he would take matters into his own hands! Or in this case his own 'feet!'

Evidently the arrangements he had made to meet someone in Springfield Road were important to him, therefore come 'hell or high water,' he was going to ensure that he would fulfil his side of that obligation. So, and in an act that at that time we all thought was 'sheer lunacy,' John decided that he would carry out a single officer 'beat' patrol, the whole way from Macrory Park down to Springfield Road!

To this very day I still find it hard to picture the scenario that played out that day. It was a really busy afternoon, with lots of vehicular and pedestrian activity taking place up and down the Whiterock and Falls Road. As we would say the place was 'hivin.'

Unquestionably, when John, who was 6ft plus, was fully kitted out in his RUC Uniform and wearing a flak jacket, he was a really imposing figure. To be frank, his character also matched that image! He was a genuinely tough guy, a gentle giant. However, for any RUC man, whether big or small, to even consider undertaking such a walk alone along that route from Macrory to Springfield Road, would have in all honesty be considered total madness.

Nevertheless, and showing immense strength of character, John defied what was the accepted norm back then and simply walked his way out of the front gate of the army base, headed down the Whiterock and onto the Falls Road, before making his way citywards and eventually arrived at Springfield Road station.

By all accounts he was at one point seen 'very casually dandering' through the crowds of shoppers on the main Falls Road, who I am sure were absolutely 'gobsmacked' at seeing this 'big peeler' greeting everyone with a cheery smile and a friendly nod of the head.

It was often said that you could get away with this sort of thing once, then the next time you tried it there would be some sort of 'terrorist welcoming party' waiting for you. I remember asking John about it and his response was typical of the man, a shrug of the shoulder, a sly smile and a bit of a laugh before he warned all who were in earshot, "don't even consider doing that, it's mad!"

Unquestionably a funny story but one that could easily have ended so differently. Just another example of one of the difficulties of not being able to drive into Springfield Road.

CHAPTER 4

Attempt to Roll Bravo Delta Eight Zero

Diary Date:	July 18, 1979.
Incident:	Attempt to roll Bravo Delta Eight Zero.
Background:	Normal Early Shift Springfield Road.
Storyteller:	Fred.

On Wednesday July 18, 1979 I was the driver of an RUC mobile patrol working the early shift (7 a.m.–3 p.m.) from Springfield Road RUC Station. Accompanied by just two other colleagues, in our entirety we were the crew of the station mobile patrol Bravo Delta Eight Zero that day. In light of the events which occurred and which I will go on to describe in detail, it's worth mentioning that our patrol vehicle was an armour-plated Land Rover, colloquially known as a Hotspur.

As the morning passed and we were approaching lunchtime, I can remember my colleague who was a woman police officer and the front seat observer that day, mentioning that she would like to get some chicken for her lunch. At this time, we were travelling country wards on the Falls Road, approaching its junction with The Whiterock Road, which was on our right.

The security situation at that time was such that most if not all of the local shops in West Belfast, wouldn't serve members of the security forces. As a consequence, we decided to head out of our own area and go across to Ballygomartin, where we would have no difficulty finding a shop which would serve us. The most natural route for that proposed journey saw us initially turn right onto the Whiterock Road, with the intention of travelling its full length, right up as far as its junction with the Springfield Road, known as Kelly's Corner. There, we would again turn right before heading cityward on Springfield Road, travelling down as far as its junction with the West Circular Road. Then it would be a short run across to the Ballygomartin Road, where we could find somewhere to buy our lunch.

As we were steadily making our way up Whiterock Road, somewhere after its junction with Ballymurphy Road but before we had reached Glenalina Road, I noticed there was a red open back lorry driving down the road towards us from the opposite direction. Bizarrely, it almost seemed to me that the lorry was deliberately veering across the central white lines of the road, but I just thought that I was imagining that!

However, as our vehicles closed on each other, it became evident that the lorry (at that time of course I didn't know if it was intentional or otherwise) was indeed headed on a collision course with our vehicle. Just before the point of impact, as the lorry was about to collide into the front driver's side area of our Land Rover, I managed to swing our vehicle violently to the left and thereby avoid a head-on collision.

The initial consequence of that swerving movement was that our vehicle took a really heavy, but mercifully glancing, blow to the front right-hand side of our vehicle. The left-hand side, our vehicles nearside, had simultaneously mounted the high kerb on our left. Whilst the force of the heavy impact rolled our vehicle up and onto its two nearside wheels, that little bit of extra leverage of having those wheels sitting fractionally higher than those on the right, proved to be just enough to prevent us from being toppled right over onto our nearside.

Inside the vehicle, which unsurprisingly had been brought to an abrupt halt by the force of the collision, we were trying to gather ourselves together, check if everyone was all right and make sense of what had just happened.

Within what was split seconds, the full reality of our predicament suddenly became shockingly clear as the noise of gunfire exploded all around us!

The first impact that I noticed, which was frighteningly heavy, struck the window of the driver's door, about six inches from my head! By then bullets were thundering off the offside of our Hotspur. The initial collision had knocked our vehicle out of gear, and despite trying my best, I was having great difficulty getting it back into any gear! Outside it seemed as if anarchy had broken out! The incoming gunfire continued unabated, and the bullets were thumping off the side armour of our vehicle! I believe there were at least three gunmen, firing from ambush points which were slightly behind us and to our right. We continued to try radioing for assistance but without success.

Somehow or other, I eventually managed to get our vehicle back into gear and moving again. It was just as I was driving away from the ambush, up the Whiterock Road, that I actually noticed there were young kids lying prostrate on the road, having dived for cover, as the prolonged attack continued. I can vividly remember seeing rounds, which had missed our vehicle, striking the high concrete wall which bordered Belfast City Cemetery on our left. The bullets were gouging deep holes in the wall!

Eventually, we were able to drive out of the immediate vicinity of the ambush, up and onto Springfield Road. Turning right we then travelled cityward, managing to 'limp' into the safety of the New Barnsley Army post. The lorry which had been used as a battering-ram by the terrorists, was later found abandoned, a little further down the Whiterock Road.

Following the incident, intelligence reports revealed just how dastardly the terrorist's plan had been for that day. Unsurprisingly, the deliberate collision by the hi-jacked lorry was to be just the initial action of this deviously planned operation, which had it been successful, would have seen the terrorist's 'wipe-out' a full crew of Police officers.

The terrorist's plan was that they would use the hijacked lorry, driven by one of their members who was seen at the time to be wearing a crash helmet, as a battering-ram. Driving down the Whiterock Road at as high a speed as he felt necessary, the driver would try to slam the lorry broadside into the slow-moving RUC vehicle, as it drove up the steep incline of the Whiterock Road. By this means they hoped the police vehicle would have been toppled over onto its side.

Had that wicked plan worked as the terrorists had anticipated, with the police vehicle stranded on its side, the floor area would naturally have been fully exposed. Its safe to say, in these circumstances, that those inside would have stood very little chance of surviving that day's gun onslaught. The floor was of course the only area of the police 'Hotspur' which back then wasn't armoured. Consequently, with the Land Rover 'turned turtle' and fully exposed, the gunmen could have taken their time to 'riddle' the unarmored floor area, causing carnage to those within the vehicle.

As time seems to stand still during these types of incidents, it's so hard to accurately assess its timescale. But I would guess that from the first shot being fired, to us escaping up the Whiterock and out of the immediate vicinity, would in reality have been no more than one or two minutes. However, take it from me, it seemed much longer!

The news media of the day reporting on this incident, record that the IRA had fired around 40 rounds at our police vehicle. The vehicle was hit multiple times in the attack. The armour-plated protection of what was known as an 'RUC Hotspur,' unquestionably saved our lives that day.

Another version of this incident

This failed attempt at mass murder appears to be of such significance that it warrants a paragraph in the book written by Ciarán de Baróid, 'Ballymurphy and The Irish War.' Describing it as another 'audacious truck attack,' he goes on to relate how a Ballymurphy ASU planned and carried out this attempt to murder the crew of an RUC patrol.

The elaborate ambush plan devised by the terrorists, had it been successful, would have seen a Police vehicle destroyed and its entire crew murdered! For this devious plan to come together, numerous stages of planning were necessary.

Initially, and undoubtedly the simplest aspect of the plans, was the need to hijack a heavy lorry for the planned ambush.

Next, they had to find a suitable house within the nearby Turf Lodge estate, which had an unobstructed view of vehicles as they travelled up and down the Whiterock Road.

Finally, when the previous requirements had been met, they would have to place numerous heavily armed gunmen at a pre-determined point on Whiterock Road.

On the day of the attempted ambush de Baróid's book reports, that once the watching IRA members noticed the Police vehicle travelling up the Whiterock Road, they signalled this fact to the driver of the lorry. On receiving his signal, the driver (apparently wearing a motorcycle helmet for protection) of the hijacked lorry then commenced his role in this machiavellian plan. Driving down the Whiterock Road he simply had to watch out for the Police Vehicle travelling towards him in the opposite direction. Then, when the opportunity arose, he was to ram his lorry directly into the oncoming Police Vehicle, creating an opportunity for the gunmen to launch their attack. Despite unleashing a torrent of heavy gunfire at the damaged Police Vehicle, with the crew protected by the vehicle's heavy armour plating, they were able to make good their escape. In de Baróid's book he mentions that 'The IRA men, who had expected the vehicle to disintegrate, melted off in disappointment.'

Postscript: Story by Andrew

The following day.

On the morning after the event described above, I was on early duty (7 a.m. – 3 p.m.) at Springfield Road RUC Station, and in attendance at a pre-duty briefing by our section Sergeant. He briefed us fully regarding the gun attack which had happened the previous day and left us in no doubt, that had it not been for the bravery and sharp driving skills of the police driver involved, things could easily have turned out very differently! The possible consequences of a Police Land Rover being 'rammed' and overturned were plainly laid out, and undoubtedly as we made our way out to our patrol vehicle, this thought was uppermost on our minds.

That morning, I was detailed to perform duty as an extra-observer in the rear of the station patrol vehicle, Bravo Delta Eight Zero. I was armed with an M1 rifle and was accompanied by two other colleagues. We left the barracks by the back gate, making our way up to Forfar Street via Cavendish Street.

Back then the large industrial plant of James Mackie & Son was located just off Forfar Street, at the bottom of Springfield Drive. We routinely patrolled that area as it was considered a possible target for terrorists, due to the fact that its workforce was mainly from the Protestant/Unionist community, in what was a predominantly Roman Catholic/Republican area.

Our vehicle continued its patrol, travelling along Forfar Street before turning right into Springfield Drive to head up towards the main Springfield Road. Approaching that junction, we got caught up in traffic forcing us to come to a stop. As our vehicle braked and came to a halt, our whole crew naturally looked out of the front windscreen to see what was causing the holdup. Literally, at that precise moment as we were all looking forward, our vehicle took what seemed to be an almighty shunt to our back end. Without a word being exchanged between us, our vehicle anti-ambush training kicked in! We immediately threw the two back doors wide open, allowing us to rapidly 'de-bus.' Almost as one, we all jumped out with our firearms raised and ready to engage any immediate threat which we might encounter!

In reality though, we were very quickly to discover that there was absolutely no threat to anyone! What had happened was nothing more than a very genuine but, in light of the previous day's incident, very badly timed accident.

One of the workers from 'Mackies,' dressed in his best 'Mackies' boilersuit and wearing a flat 'cap,' had been driving his works forklift truck up Springfield Drive towards the main road. Basically, he was following us. But somehow or other he hadn't noticed that the vehicle ahead of him, us, had come to a sudden stop.

The upshot of his carelessness was that he ran his forklift truck, smack into the back of our armour-plated Hotspur. The poor man was literally three or four feet from the back doors of the Land Rover, when (at that time anyway) three fairly young and reasonably fit policemen exploded out from the vehicles back doors, with their guns literally trained on him! You should have seen his 'wee face!'

When the dust had settled and we all came down from 'forty thousand feet,' we took time to apologise for our seeming overreaction to what was nothing more than a very minor road traffic accident. Indeed, on closer examination there was little or no damage to either vehicle, so we were all able to continue with our days' work as if nothing had happened.

I often wonder what that unfortunate forklift driver, on his return to the factory, told his workmates about his brief but no doubt 'dramatic encounter,' with what in all honesty was a very nervy RUC crew that day!

CHAPTER 5

Sniper Ambush at the Royal Victoria Hospital

Diary Date:	September 20, 1979.
Incident:	IRA Sniper Attack, within Grounds of Royal Victoria Hospital.
Background:	Normal Early Shift Springfield Road.
Storyteller:	Billy.

Around 6:45 a.m. on the morning of Thursday, September 20, 1979, I reported for duty at Springfield Road RUC Station, along with my other 'D' Section colleagues. We paraded in the briefing room as was normal, where we were each given our roles for that day's duty. I was detailed to be the observer in the station's main patrol vehicle, Bravo Delta Eight Zero. Unusually though, just as we thought the briefing was over, our section Sergeant gave us some additional information, which had been passed to our authorities from the RUC Special Branch. They reported that they had received intelligence which seemed to indicate that there was going to be some sort of attack on the Police that day, by members of the IRA. They weren't able to elaborate on that fairly basic piece of information, but they did say that there was a possibility that the attack may take place somewhere on the grounds of the Royal Victoria Hospital (RVH).

Whilst grateful for the Special Branch 'heads up,' unfortunately at that time in our country's history, the threat of an IRA attack on the Police in West Belfast, was hardly a groundbreaking piece of intelligence!

Nonetheless, with this additional bit of information stowed away, our two Land Rover crews gathered ourselves together and headed out to patrol the area. I remember that morning we had an Inspector out in the vehicle with us, sitting in what police officers' term as the observer's seat. Ie, the front passenger's seat. As a consequence, I took up a seat in the rear of the vehicle with the other members of our crew.

The morning passed by uneventfully until around 9:30 a.m., when we received a radio transmission to the effect that a damage only Road Traffic Accident (RTA) had just occurred outside what was known as the 'geriatric' unit in the Royal. Needless to say, this had us thinking back to the earlier briefing and the report that there may be an attack on the Police within the grounds of the RVH.

Unusually, our crew voiced their concerns regarding attending this accident. The consensus was that if the incident was indeed a genuine damage only RTA, then those involved could exchange their details, and let the insurance companies sort out the damage. However, if it wasn't a genuine accident, and one which had been staged as a 'come on,' to draw the police in for an attack, we would be better off staying clear.

Our Inspector, who I seem to remember was fairly new to the area, was of a different opinion though. He felt that it would be safe enough for our two vehicles to take a drive through the main road, which runs through the Royal grounds, and once there we could better assess whether or not we should attend the scene.

So, against what everyone else felt to be the right thing to do, we made our way into the Royal complex. As we passed along the main road, we were able to see that a vehicle had indeed run into the rear of a parked car just outside the Geriatric Unit. We also noted that a nurse was standing at the door of the unit and at least one other person was with her, possibly a member of the RVH security. For better or worse the decision was then taken to stop the vehicles and attend the call. Both Land Rover crews quickly debussed, with members taking up covering positions around the area.

As vehicle observer, and the officer whose responsibility it now was to deal with the accident, clipboard in hand, I walked down towards the nurse. She informed me that the car parked in the designated car park bay was hers, and that the driver of the other car which had mysteriously collided into the back of hers, had left the scene.

On hearing what the nurse had said and looking at the odd positioning of the vehicle which had run into the back of her car, I have to say that a cold chill ran through my body. The hairs on the back of my neck stood up, as things just didn't seem right. It seemed to me that for the nurse's car to be hit from that angle, the moving car would almost have had to have made that manoeuvre deliberately! It appeared that it would have been significantly harder for the driver of the offending vehicle to have struck the nurse's static car in that way, than it would have been for him to have driven past it!

Suddenly my worst fears were realised! Just then the blast of two loud piercing cracks sounded out! The noise seemed to reverberate around the area of low ground, where the Geriatric Unit was located! Easily identified as being from some sort of high-velocity rifle, myself and my colleagues dived to the ground for cover. One of our crew almost immediately shouted out that he had identified the firing point, which he pointed out was a rear window in a small terrace house on Thames Street.

As soon as we had clarified that no police officer or members of the public had been hit, we raced back to our vehicles. Just as quickly as we could, we then made our way round to Thames Street. Needless to say, by then the gunmen had made their escape.

Postscript

A follow up CID investigation revealed that two members of the IRA had entered that small, terraced house in Thames Street sometime earlier. Holding the two elderly residents' captive, the terrorists then set about putting into motion what they believed was a well thought out plan to ambush the police. The follow up operation revealed that those involved in this scheme had been there for some time, as there were enough food wrappers, drinks bottles and cigarette butts found at the firing point, to indicate that was the case.

I mentioned earlier that this ambush appears to have been a well thought out plan. However, in retrospect it does seem that the only thing which saved us that day, was in actuality, bad planning on the part of the terrorists!

Let me explain.

The theory of this planned shooting of Police, whilst they were in attendance at a deliberately staged road traffic accident, certainly appeared to be foolproof. The concealed firing position gave the gunmen a great vantage point, which overlooked the area where the terrorists believed they could easily lure the police. Additionally, it was outside the actual grounds of the Royal, meaning that after the shoot it would take the police or indeed any military support crew, perhaps ten minutes or more to make their way round to Thames Street. Giving them plenty of time to complete their escape.

The real problem of this sniper attack, which seems to have been lost in the terrorists planning of this attempt to murder police, was in the actual 'topography' of the area. Or to be even more specific, the unforeseen complication lay in the 'dead ground,' which was between the firing point and the area where they planned their potential targets would be.

Back then the specific area where this incident occurred, was quite different to what it is nowadays. The area of the Royal grounds which lay immediately at the rear of that house in Thames Street, was a fairly substantial, tarmac car park. This car park sat at a higher level than both the main road which ran through the Royal, and even more so than the site of the Royal's Geriatric Unit, which was at a lower level again than the main through road.

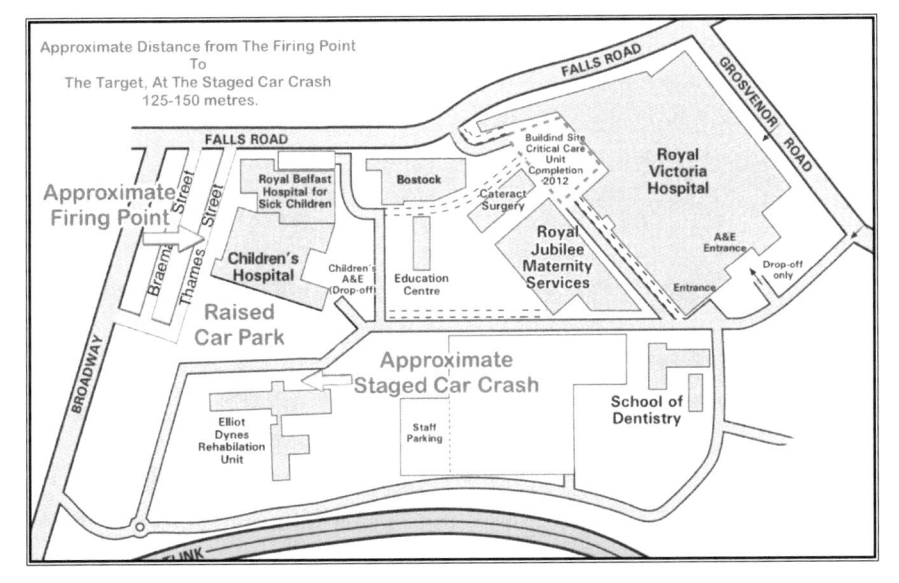

Map of Royal Showing Relevant Locations

In essence the area of 'dead ground' that the terrorists had to shoot over, included both the raised car park and then the main road. Both of which were at higher levels, than the lower-level Geriatric Unit. It appears that when the plans for this shoot were made, the car park was empty, meaning there was an unobstructed view of the potential target area.

However, on the day of the actual shoot, the car park was in use and was well-filled with cars. As a consequence, that planned unobstructed shot of approximately 125-150 metres, was no longer available to the terrorist gunman! His two shots from his covert firing position in Thames Street, had to be directed through the windscreen of a car, which was parked in that raised park. Thankfully, the windscreen deflected both of the aimed shots off target, and it seems that they actually went high above our heads.

CHAPTER 6

M60 Double Murder at Springfield Road Station.

Diary Date:	October 28, 1979.
Incident:	M60 murder of Constable Gerry Davidson & Warrant Officer David Bellamy.
Background:	Normal Early Shift Springfield Road.
Storyteller:	Andrew.

In the chronicle of the Northern Ireland Troubles, 1979 was a particularly bleak year. The records indicate that there were 120 Troubles-related deaths that year, a high which thankfully was never seen again. Seventy-six of those deaths are recorded as having been members of the Security Forces. (Army, Police, Prison Staff)

To be more specific about events around the time of this particular incident, security force intelligence reported that a particularly infamous IRA Active Service Unit was in operation in the Greater Belfast area. They carried the nickname of being the 'M60 Gun Team' or 'The M60 Gang,' as one part of their weaponry was a heavy M60 machine gun. Nicknamed 'The Pig,' because of its voracious appetite for ammunition, the belt-fed American built M60 is capable of firing 600 armour-piercing rounds per minute. Even to a gun novice like me, it's clear that this was a gun designed and manufactured for use in open battlefield conditions, certainly not for use in inner-city streets.

Police briefings at the time left us in no doubt as to the considerable threat this experienced and ruthless four-to-five-man IRA ASU carried. During this period, they had been involved in numerous fatal hit-and-run gun attacks on both the Army and the Police. A fuller explanation of those involved in this particular IRA unit is readily available on the internet. A simple search for 'IRA M60 Gun team' will turn up ample information, should anyone wish to do so.

This may seem to be a really obscure manner to commence this particular story, but this is just the way I remember it. For those reading this and worrying over its relevance to these police memoirs, I'm sure as the story progresses it will become increasingly clear to you as we go along.

Back in the day, football supporters like me were really restricted in what TV coverage was available. Besides big games such as FA Cup Finals or important international matches, we had to make do with two one-hour highlight programmes per week. On Saturday evenings, there was the BBC offering of 'Match of The Day,' and on Sunday afternoon, ITV's 'The Big Match.' The First Division fixtures on Saturday, October 27, 1979, included Spurs playing Nottingham Forest in a match at White Hart Lane, London. Out of interest, Spurs won that match through a spectacular volleyed goal by the then up and coming English football superstar, Glen Hoddle.

On the afternoon of the following day, along with two other colleagues, I reported for duty at Springfield Road. The three of us proceeded to ready ourselves for that day's duty, as we gathered together the usual firearms, ammunition, and flak-jackets, which of course were the norm at that time.

Once organised we made our way out into the station yard, where the fleet of station Land Rovers would routinely be parked. It quickly became evident that the parking area was virtually empty, with only one vehicle present. That being the situation, we went ahead and mustered our gear into that vehicle. I jumped into the driver's seat and slowly edged the Rover towards the front gate of the station, which was manned by military personnel. As we waited for one of the soldiers to emerge from his 'sangar' and open the heavily fortified front gate for us, another policeman appeared from the station and started calling to us. He explained that the vehicle which we were then driving was their patrol's vehicle, and as such it wasn't available for us to use. So, I simply reversed away from the now half-opened front gates, parked the vehicle, gathered up our gear, and went back into the station.

As there was no other vehicle available for our patrol, we retired to the station Recreation Room. I use the title 'Recreation Room' very loosely in this case! The reality was that back then, our recreation facilities didn't amount to very much. They consisted of one fairly dark office/room, which due to having solid armour-plated windows, never saw any natural light. A series of fairly basic soft seats lined the walls and there was a couple of low coffee tables in the middle of the room, which always seemed to be heavily laden with overflowing ashtrays!

Anyway, as I mentioned previously it was Sunday afternoon and the 'Big Match' was on the telly, so we quickly settled down to watch the highlights of the previous day's game. We were enjoying the match and eulogising over Hoddle's wonderful goal, when suddenly our peaceful afternoon was shockingly and fearfully interrupted, by a noise that I'd never heard before or since.

Even though we were deep inside the safety of the police barracks, the thunderous noise of very heavy gunfire totally engulfed us! One of my two colleagues, who was an ex-soldier, immediately identified the source of the noise to us. "That's an M60," he yelled at the top of his voice.

M60 Machine Gun

The three of us immediately sprang to our feet, dashing out into the front yard to investigate what had actually happened. We hadn't stopped to take the time to put on our flak jackets or to grab any additional firearms, so were only lightly armed, each with our personal protection weapons, Walther PPKs.

The large fortified double gates of the station were at this point lying wide open and were seemingly unmanned! The gunfire had by then stopped, creating an eerie silence and there were no immediate signs of any casualties, damage, or threat!

Then one of the soldiers who was on security duty inside the sangar, screamed to us that the RUC mobile vehicle which had just left the station, had been caught up in an ambush. He elaborated that although it had been badly hit, it had somehow managed to falteringly drive away from the immediate vicinity of the ambush, in a citywards direction on the Springfield Road. The three of us, then foolishly ran out onto the main road in a vain hope of engaging the terrorists.

Thankfully though, by the time we arrived at the scene, the terrorists who were much heavier armed than we were, had completed their evil attack and by then were making their escape. Eventually reinforcements of police and army personnel flooded the area, enabling our detectives to carry out a full and detailed investigation into the events of that fateful afternoon.

It seems that sometime earlier that day, at least four members of the previously mentioned IRA M60 Gun team, entered and 'took over' a house at the junction of Crocus Street and Springfield Road. The precise position of this house made it particularly attractive to the terrorists, as its two first-floor windows overlooked the front gate of Springfield Road RUC station.

The view the terrorist gunmen would have had of Springfield Road, before launching the gun attack.

A seemingly ideal location, which besides enabling them to observe the routine comings and goings at the front of the police station, also meant that right up to the very moment they launched their attack, they would remain unseen. They came prepared for the ambush and were heavily armed, with a couple of rifles in addition to the heavy calibre M60 machine gun.

Once in position, all they had to do was sit back and wait for the right opportunity to launch their deadly attack. It seems that that opportunity arrived just a minute or two after we had handed over the vehicle to our colleagues inside the station.

For some unknown reason, our replacement crew chose to reverse the Hotspur out of the front gate. To provide armed cover for this manoeuvre and ensure safe passage out from the front of the station and onto the Springfield Road, the crew deployed a couple of members on foot. They were also joined by a colleague from the military, Warrant Officer David Bellamy of the Duke of Wellington Regiment.

Giving armed cover and helping to direct the reversing vehicle out of the station, the RUC Sergeant shouted instructions to the driver before again approaching the vehicle, to climb back on board. As soon as the rear double doors of the now static Land Rover were opened to let their colleagues back into the vehicle, the gunmen launched their deadly ambush! Frighteningly, in what was in all probability an attack which lasted no more than 10-15 seconds, they fired around 50 rounds at the static and now very vulnerable target.

All three who were in the rear of the vehicle were hit, as well as the RUC Sergeant sitting in the front passenger seat. Sustaining the worst possible injuries, Warrant Officer Bellamy died almost immediately and was pronounced dead on arrival at the RVH. The police Constable who had been in the rear of the vehicle with him, Gerry Davidson, also sustained life-threatening gunshot wounds. He had been hit in the head and neck, but miraculously was still alive when the badly shot-up vehicle made it to the nearby Royal Victoria Hospital. He was immediately treated for his injuries and eventually put on a life support machine. Sadly though, some three weeks later Gerry lost his fight for life, as he succumbed to the injuries sustained in the attack. Fortunately, the story regarding the Sergeant had a much happier outcome. Despite being hit on no less than seven occasions and also spending time on a life support machine, after many months of treatment and rehabilitation, he was able to make a complete recovery from his injuries. Indeed, he went on to have a full and rewarding career in the RUC.

Ambush victim dies on life-support machine
Shot RUC man loses battle for his life

AN RUC constable who had been on a life-support machine for the past three weeks, after he was gunned down in an IRA ambush in West Belfast, died in hospital yesterday.
Constable Gerry Davidson (26), father of two young children, was seriously injured with head and neck wounds when the Land-Rover in which he was a passenger came under fire while leaving Springfield Road Police Station in West Belfast on October 28.
A soldier — Warrant Officer David Bellamy (31), of the Army Physical Training Corps — was shot dead and an RUC sergeant seriously injured in the ambush which was laid by gunmen operating from a house at Crocus Street, overlooking the police station.
Last night an RUC spokesman said the sergeant was progressing satisfactorily.

LEFT: Constable Gerry Davidson, Age 26. Father of two young children.

Right: Warrant Officer David Bellamy, Age 31.

Newspaper cutting

Postscript

Whilst still at the scene of the attack and carrying out my duties as Log Scene Officer, we were eventually joined at the scene by members of our own section, including our Sergeant. I'll never forget that the first words he spoke to me that day, were words of disapproval! He seemed to enjoy pointing out, that at that time I wasn't wearing my police cap!

CHAPTER 7

Member Isolated on Foot in Hostile Area

Diary Date:	Early November, 1979.
Incident:	Officer Unwittingly Stranded on Foot.
Background:	Normal Night Shift Springfield Road.
Storyteller:	Billy.

This story relates to an incident in which I was involved, way back in November 1979. Considering just how close this came to being an absolute disaster, it may seem surprising that I can't be definitive about the exact date. My official notebooks from that era are now long gone, so I simply have no way of being able to tie the date down. Whilst the actual date may have been lost in the ether of time, the events of that evening are well and truly etched into my memory! Even though it happened 45 years ago, the trauma and shock of that evening still live with me on a daily basis.

That evening, around 10:45 p.m., along with my 'D' Section colleagues, I reported for night shift at Springfield Road station. At our pre-duty briefing, our Inspector assigned the duties for each section member. My particular role that night, was to act as the driver of our station mobile patrol vehicle, callsign Bravo Delta Eight Zero. Our crew was made up of a woman police Constable as our front seat observer, and two other police Constables acting as extra observers. They would ride in the back of our armour-plated Hotspur for the duration of our shift.

As we were making our way out to the station yard, we were informed by our radio control room that a stolen Ford Capri car had been seen driving up and down the Falls Road, near to the rear of our station.

Due to the lack of space within the station complex, Springfield Road station had a one-way system in operation. The norm, of course there were exceptions, was that operational vehicles would enter the station by the front gate, and then leave it via the back gate.

At that time, on exiting the back gate, there was an area outside the station of about 50 metres before you would reach the junction with Cavendish Street. (See photo of Springfield Road 'Back Gate' in Section 1.) In light of the reports that a stolen Ford Capri car had been seen; I decided to stop our vehicle in that area, just short of the Cavendish Street junction. There, we could sit unseen and see any cars which travelled from the main Falls Road along Cavendish Street and the back of our station. It seemed that we had only just pulled-up when low and behold, the stolen silver Ford Capri drove past.

Conscious that a Capri in any of the many guises in which Ford produced it, would easily outrun our very heavy armoured Hotspur in a chase, without putting our vehicle's 'two-tones or blue-light' on, I eased our vehicle out onto Cavendish Street and followed it. Surprisingly, it was travelling quite slowly as it made a left hand turn off Cavendish Street and onto Oakman Street, which led down towards Beechmount Avenue and the Falls Road.

Experience told me that the majority of stolen cars in that area at that time, was generally the work of what was colloquially known as 'Joyriders!' This was a description of a practice normally carried out by local teenagers, who stole a car simply to take it for a reckless and speedy drive around the area, before just abandoning them.

In this instance and indeed most unusually, this 'stollie' continued driving at a very sedate pace, as it headed down Beechmount Avenue in the general direction of the Falls Road. Its lack of speed enabled me to accelerate our vehicle out around the Ford, before immediately pulling across its front and blocking it's escape route.

Our crew jumped out and quickly detained all those who were in the stolen car. As expected, those we apprehended were nothing more than five or six local kids, who having stolen the car were now participating in and enjoying a bit of 'joyriding.' Albeit quite slowly!

Viewed as a real anti-social practice within the local communities, joyriding was deeply frowned upon by the paramilitaries. Indeed, there is a long history of paramilitary organisations routinely handing out 'summary justice,' to those whom they believe have been guilty of such crimes. Their perception of justice however is beyond the scope of any rational thinking person. Punishments routinely dispensed by the paramilitary groupings can range from 'a cuff round the ear' or a 'bit of a beating,' right up to being shot! In reality, the kids we arrested should have considered themselves very lucky that it was us and not the paramilitaries who had detained them!

Thankfully, we had managed to get the vehicle stopped before it had made its way out and onto the main Falls Road. The benefit of this was that there would be less chance of encountering the attention of any 'rent-a-crowd,' a phenomenon for which the Falls area is particularly notorious!

Beechmount Avenue and its surrounding area, whilst every bit as hostile to the police as the Falls, was at that time of night considerably quieter. Understandably so, as by this time it was around midnight, there was little or no pedestrian or vehicular traffic about, so we were able to carry on our duties unhindered. We did note however that none of the streetlights were working, which gave the area a particularly dark and sinister ambience!

We continued with our responsibilities, informing control that we had stopped the stolen vehicle and arrested its occupants. We then loaded all the youths into the rear of our Land Rover for transport round to Springfield Road Station, which was little more than a couple of minutes away.

To ensure the stolen car wouldn't get re-stolen and since we knew there was no likelihood of it being boobytrapped, we concluded that in this instance it would be safe enough to bring it back to the station with us. One of our crew would replace me as driver of our patrol vehicle, whilst I would drive the stolen car back to our base.

The Land Rover crew then mounted up, and now fully loaded with all of those who we had arrested, headed down Beechmount Avenue towards the Falls Road. The intention was that they would turn left onto the Falls and head back to the station that way, with me tucked in closely behind in the stolen car. As they drove off, I confidently reached down towards where I fully expected to find the car's key, in the vehicle's ignition.

However, I suddenly realised that there was no key in the ignition and a quick check confirmed my worst fear, the Capri which was of course now not running, had been hot-wired! There seemed to be wires sticking out everywhere, leaving me with absolutely no idea how to get the car running again. By the time the reality of my situation struck home, the Land Rover was some distance away, and it seemed that none of my colleagues were aware of what was happening! I remember vividly seeing the brake lights of our vehicle coming on, just as the driver slowed on approaching the Falls Road. I watched, almost pleadingly, as it turned left and disappeared out of sight in a city ward's direction.

The reality of my immediate predicament hit me like a sledgehammer! I was alone and isolated in what was a really hostile area for police, with absolutely no means of contacting my colleagues or calling for help! I seem to remember thinking to myself, or did I actually say it out loud, "what the hell am I going to do now?"

Worth pointing out at this juncture, is the fact that back then the standard operational procedure in Springfield Road was that anyone who was detailed to drive the station mobile patrol vehicle, would not sign out and carry a personal radio. They would however sign a SMG or an M1 Rifle out of the armoury to enhance the crew's security.

I have never considered myself to be skittish or cowardly in any way, but this was unquestionably one instance in my life that I really wanted the ground to open-up and swallow me! I was angry, I was frightened, and I was really frustrated, all in one!

I can vividly remember standing back into the darkened shadows of the high wall which ran down that part of Beechmount Avenue and trying to take stock of my situation! As I looked around, it appeared that most of the nearby houses were by this time in darkness. This ruled out my initial idea, of simply knocking on someone's door and asking to use their phone!

Then it struck me that there was a small shop near to the Beechmount Avenue junction on the Falls Road, which kept really late hours. So, armed with a station issue Sterling Machine Gun, and also having my personal protection Walther pistol concealed in its holster, I gingerly started to edge my way down Beechmount towards the Falls.

As I continued to edge my way down towards the main road, I remember feeling an almost overwhelming sense of isolation! The area, as I mentioned earlier was in darkness, creating a particularly eerie and frighteningly still ambiance. My survival instincts and senses were at this point in overdrive, as each little sound I heard or any perceived movement that caught my eye, saw me dropping down to one knee to take up a defensive firing position, with my back firmly anchored against the nearest wall!

I eventually made it down to the main road and to my relief noticed that the shop lights were still on, indicating that it was open. Before crossing,

I quickly glanced up and down the Falls, noting that it seemed unusually quiet. Deliberately, I took a few seconds to calm myself down before stepping into the small shop. Once inside, I was met by a shopkeeper, who by the look on his face was almost terror-stricken by the presence of an armed RUC man standing in his shop at that time of night.

Similarly, at this point I was feeling a bit like the proverbial 'rabbit caught in a car's headlights,' but I did pluck up the courage to ask him if I could make use of his shop's phone? With what seemed like a large element of loathing in his voice, he aggressively replied that there wasn't a phone on the premises. To this day I don't know if that was the case or not. As I look back now, I can't believe that I took that immediate negative response at face value! I didn't even repeat the question, before turning and almost in a sheepish manner, walked towards the door.

It was just then, as I was about to leave the shop and having looked out onto what was a relatively well-lit section of the Falls Road, that I realised my predicament had changed somewhat. It had got worse! Somehow or other the local 'rent a crowd,' which always seemed to appear at the worst possible time, had mysteriously materialised and were gathered around the door of the shop. There were about a dozen or so teenagers standing in a semicircle around the door, making it impossible for me to simply walk away! My heart was racing, as I plucked up the courage to tell them to move aside! Needless to say, they ignored repeated requests/warnings to that effect. The false bravado they showed in openly defying my instructions, was I believe in part down to the 'Dutch Courage' they had found in the bottles of alcohol that they were holding.

Not knowing what else to do, and honestly being in fear for my life, I decided that I would cock the Sterling and fire a few rounds up in the air, in an attempt to scatter the crowd. I pulled the cocking handle back, lifted the Sterling up to my shoulder and aimed it high into the air. I then pulled the trigger, fully confident that the gun would rattle off a few unaimed but hopefully noisy shots, which would maybe just buy me a bit of time to escape. As expected, the block of the firing mechanism then flew forward, but unbelievably it didn't fire! I was absolutely horrified!

But just before any of the watching crowd could react to the guns malfunction, the natural physiological human response of 'fight or flight' kicked in! Without thinking, I suddenly put my head down and ran straight at the youths, barging my way through them before darting away just as fast as I could. I sprinted across some open waste ground, which was heavily littered with rubble, before emerging onto the main Falls Road, and continued to run in a citywards direction.

This totally unplanned action seemed to surprise them, almost as much as it did me! It took them a few seconds to realise that their quarry had escaped. Once they gathered themselves, they started chasing me over the waste ground. Throwing bricks and bottles, which they must have picked up as they ran, they continued their noisy pursuit. I was really struggling to stay ahead of them. The additional weight of my flak-jacket and guns seemed to weigh a ton, as I just kept trying to run as fast as I could!

As I neared the traffic lights at the top of Broadway, I noticed a Police Hotspur sitting at that junction, waiting to turn right onto the Falls. I screamed, shouted, and waved at them in the vain hope they would see me and stop their vehicle! But they hadn't noticed, as when the lights turned, they continued their journey down the Falls, seemingly without giving me a second thought.

With the 'baying mob' still nipping at my heels, I had reached the point on the Falls Road where it is intersected with Broadway. This busy junction is also the location of an extremely popular bar which at this time of night was likely to be getting busy with people leaving those premises. Obviously, this would be the last thing that I would want! It was just then I noticed there was a single car stopped at the traffic lights, waiting for the lights to change before continuing on down the Falls Road. In what wasn't an overly thought-out plan I lunged towards it. Just as it was about to move off, I banged on its roof and the driver stopped his vehicle. I threw open the near-side back door and dived headlong into the backseat.

I really wasn't in a good way at this point! I was out of breath from the chase, sweating profusely and mentally, I was almost in a state of blind panic. Withdrawing my Walther from its holster, and with a very shaky hand I pointed the gun directly at the driver. I demanded that he drive off just as quickly as possible, and that he should head directly to Springfield Road police station.

The alarmed driver, despite having a gun shoved in his face by a policeman who was clearly in a heightened state of anxiety, somehow managed to remain calm. Seemingly quite unruffled by the experience, he replied that he would do that, no problem! He accelerated his car away from the junction just as the chasing crowd arrived, but thankfully they were just too late to hinder my escape as we made our way down the Falls.

In just a couple of minutes we pulled up at the heavily fortified front gates of Springfield Road station. I quickly jumped out, doubtless leaving the poor driver somewhat bewildered as to what had just happened! He drove off country-wards on the Springfield Road, just as a soldier who would have seen us from the station security sangar, ran out of the station and ushered me in through the main gates.

Feeling rather perplexed by what had just happened, I let him escort me into the station through a doorway which would generally only ever be used by members of the public. Consequently, when I made my unexpected appearance back into the station through this door, my colleagues who were just then readying themselves to send out a search party, were completely astonished as I appeared out of nowhere! It was evident that on the realisation that I was missing, the station had gone into full panic mode! The resident army battalion had already scrambled its QRF,[4] Quick Reaction Force, who were by then on route to the Beechmount area.

My own vehicle crew, who just ten minutes earlier had inadvertently left me stranded in the Beechmount, were all standing there looking uncomfortable and shamefaced! In an uncontrolled rage, I let each of them know just exactly what I thought of them. In truth, if I hadn't been held back by others, I would most likely have ended up punching them.

However, having been escorted away from the immediate area and given some very comforting and sage words of advice by our Inspector, I was eventually able to cool down. Our Divisional Commander, who was actually in the station that night and who was part of the 'search party,' then summoned me up to his office. I have to say that at his behest, we spent a couple of hours chatting whilst I drank just enough of his whisky to enable me to get some much-needed sleep.

Purely for medicinal purposes of course!

Postscript

As I returned to duty over the succeeding days, I fully expected to hear how some member of the public had reported how he had been hijacked at gunpoint by a seemingly out of control policeman. To the best of my knowledge that driver never reported the incident to the Police.

The eventual outcome of that night could so easily have been very different! Indeed, to this very day, I still struggle with the repercussions of it.

---

4 The Military or Police QRF, would have been a group of soldiers/police, who whilst remaining within their barracks and ostensibly off-duty, would always have to be ready to respond at a moment's notice. Almost like the Fire Brigade. No set strength, but generally 8-12 members.

CHAPTER 8

House Fire in Andersonstown

Diary Date:	January 11, 1980.
Incident:	Family rescued in Andersonstown.
Background:	Normal Early Shift.
Storyteller:	Andrew.

On the morning of Friday, January 11, 1980, I reported for the early shift at Springfield Road RUC Station. At our pre duty briefing I was detailed by my section sergeant to undertake the role of extra observer in the stations main patrol vehicle, Bravo Delta Eight Zero.

That morning due to other commitments, our crew was particularly light in number, with only three of us in the vehicle. Once we got ourselves organised, we moved out of the station and commenced our patrol in the normal manner. I remember that almost as soon as we had left the station, our driver mentioned that he had a follow-up 'call' to make, to a house which was just outside our own area. As we had just commenced our shift, this would have been around 7 a.m., hence his reasoning that he would put off the call until around 8 a.m., before waking up the whole household.

Back then the practice was that any patrol vehicle which was planning on leaving their own area, would be required to seek permission to do so, from the radio control room in Springfield Road, Bravo Delta. So around 8 a.m. we informed control of our request and subsequently received permission to travel the short distance to Denewood Park. I seem to remember that this was a fairly quiet, small street in Andersonstown.

We subsequently made our way along the Falls Road to the Andersonstown area, where we located the address that our driver was looking for. On arrival, he mentioned that his task would probably take five or ten minutes. Then he and our observer left the vehicle and headed across to the house where the call was. To give them proper cover, I took up a position whereby I could see them, and also keep an eye on any threat from the immediate area.

I had only settled into my covering position, when from a house that was maybe 50 yards away from where I was kneeling, I noticed a man fleeing and he was literally enveloped in a cloud of black smoke! From my initial position, I couldn't be definite, but it almost seemed as if his hair was on fire! He was frantically patting his head, seemingly trying to extinguish flames.

Whilst very conscious that my primary role was to provide security cover for my two colleagues, this man's emergency situation demanded that I should go to his aid immediately.

As I ran toward the house, the closer I got the more desperate the situation appeared! The injured party, whilst at that point not actually on fire, had clearly just left an area which had been! He was swathed from head to foot in soot and smoke! He was screaming frantically that his family were still upstairs in his home, and that it was on fire! There seemed to be smoke billowing out of every door and window. I tried to calm him down and asked how many of his family were left in the house, and exactly where they would be within the building. He told me that his wife was still inside along with their four kids, and that they would be upstairs in their bedrooms. I then turned away from him and made my way through the open front door of the house. However, almost immediately, I became aware that the householder had actually followed me back into the building. Literally just as I had commenced feeling my way around the walls inside the front door, I could feel him holding on to my back! Given the distressed state he was in, it was clear that he was in no fit state to continue, so I quickly took him back outside and told him to seek out my two colleagues who were just down the street.

Unsurprisingly the inside of the house was dense with smoke, which made vision almost impossible. But thankfully by getting onto all fours, I was able to make my way upstairs and once there locate the man's family. We quickly got some cloths and covered our mouths and noses. Then, hand in hand, we made our way down the stairs and out of the house, where the family had a tearful reunion. I made my way around the back of the house and managed to get in through the back door, before locating and extinguishing the fire.

A short time later the Fire Service arrived and took control of the incident, whilst we boarded up our Land Rover and headed back into our area.

> **RUC man saves four in fire drama**
>
> A 21-YEAR-OLD police constable rescued a woman and her three children from a fire in their Andersonstown home early today.
>
> The policeman was a member of a mobile patrol which noticed smoke coming from a house at Denewood Park.
>
> As they approached the house, they met the husband who told them that his wife and three children were asleep upstairs.
>
> The man tried to get upstairs but was beaten back by the dense smoke. The young constable then managed to reach the bedrooms and bring the woman and children to safety.
>
> He then went around to the back of the house, broke down the door and extinguished the blaze before the fire brigade arrived.
>
> An RUC spokesman said it appeared that the fire had started accidentally, and rapidly got out of control.
>
> *Belfast Telegraph, Friday, January 11, 1980.*

Postscript

Northern Ireland's two main daily newspapers, the Belfast Telegraph and the News Letter ran this story in their pages the following day. The accidental fire had started when the father of the family had been trying to light the main fire in the house. To this end he had tried spraying some sort of accelerant into the hearth, but somehow or other the actual container holding the liquid, had ignited. With the bottle of accelerant now ablaze, the householder then attempted to get outside where he could dispose of the immediate danger.

Unfortunately, just as he was crossing the living room he tripped, spraying the accelerant all over the carpeted floor. The carpets burst into flame, creating an inferno that engulfed him whilst he lay prone on the ground. With his hair now on fire, he ran out of the house and into the road, which is when I first saw him.

Some days after the incident I was called to the Divisional Commanders Office, along with my section Inspector. They commended me on the role I'd played in this incident and then surprised me by handing me a small letter. (A copy of which I have to this day.) On opening the letter, I was somewhat taken aback when I realised it had been written by the mother of the house. In a few short lines she kindly expressed her gratitude for the help she and her family had received from the Police that day. She had no idea who I was, but she had simply addressed it to our authorities and handed it over the counter at Andersonstown RUC station, sure in the knowledge that they would be able to identify who the officer involved had been.

Besides some genuine words of appreciation, the lady had included a small sum of money, which she wanted me to have as a token of her appreciation. I expressed just how reluctant I was to accept this very kind but totally unnecessary gesture, but my two senior officers both felt that for me to refuse this token of the lady's appreciation, could be construed as being ungrateful, consequently, they encouraged me to keep the gift.

Below: A copy of the letter I received from the Andersonstown family.

> Dear Sir,
>
> On Friday 11·1·80 at 7.15 AM, we had an accident in our house resulting in a fire,
>
> Two of immediatly appeared at the scene wasted no time in getting the Brigade, from the bottom of my heart I wish to thank these men as we all know the situation in our Country and as they didn't know who or what we were, they put their own lives in danger to make sure that we were all safe and well and after that, they

did their utmost to protect the property, one went out the back and helped put the fire out. I will be forever grateful to these valiant men and I have them to thank for my four children being safe and well to-night. I do not know their names but I have no doubt you will investigate who they were and pass on to them once again my heartfelt thanks

Yours faithfully.

```
                    POLICE AUTHORITY FOR NORTHERN IRELAND
                    5th Floor, River House
                    48 High Street, BELFAST BT1 2DR
    Telephone Belfast 30111
```

Our Reference: LD 10/5
Date *14 October 1980*

Dear *Constable*

I wish to confirm the arrangements which have been made with you for the presentation of the Royal Humane Society Awards in the Conference Room, 7th Floor, River House, on Thursday *27 November 1980* at 3.00 pm.

I look forward to meeting you and would ask that you complete and return the portion below as soon as possible stating the number of guests who will be attending with you, plus details of your car should you require a car park space in the Authority's car park.

Yours sincerely

(Miss)

In November of that year, I received an award from the 'Protection of Life from Fire Society' to mark my efforts on that day.

CHAPTER 9

An Encounter with an Assassin.

Diary Date:	January 17th, 1980.
Incident:	Suspicious Object Falls Road Library.
Background:	Normal Early Shift.
Storyteller:	Andrew.

At 6:30 a.m. on Thursday January 17, 1980, I paraded for duty at Springfield Road RUC Station. My own section sergeant detailed our crews that morning and I was detailed to carry out the duties of the main vehicle observer, in Bravo Delta Eight Zero.

At 9:35 a.m. we received a radio message from our control room to the effect that a report had just been received from the staff at the Falls Road Library, in which they said that they believed they had discovered a suspicious object/parcel, on their premises. Further, they said that this object seemed to be attached to the base of the library's flagpole, which was on the building's balcony area. The flag which was hanging from the flagpole that morning was the Irish Tricolour [5].

---

5   The Irish Tricolour is the flag of the Republic of Ireland, not of Northern Ireland. It is a symbol readily identified by those within the Northern Ireland community who would retain aspirations of a United Ireland. The majority of this country's population, however, remain committed to the the Union of Northern Ireland and Great Britain. As such, the flying of the tricolour can be a very divisive matter in Northern Ireland.

Balcony at Falls Road Library

When we arrived at the library, my Sergeant who was in the patrol vehicle that day, and I made our way inside to chat to the staff. They confirmed to us that whilst the library did have an official flagpole in the balcony, the tricolour flag which had mysteriously appeared overnight, was unofficial and had nothing to do with the library or its staff.

They escorted us upstairs and showed us the location of the balcony, where the flagpole was located. Without getting too close, we were able to see that there was indeed something either attached to or sitting very close to the base of the flagpole. We also noted there were coloured electrical wires attached to the package.

Now, to be brutally honest as we discussed our next actions, both my Sergeant and I felt very sure that this was nothing more than an elaborate hoax. However, we were also very conscious that in the past, IRA terrorists had attached booby-trap bombs to flagpoles in the hope that members of the security forces would detonate the bomb, as they tried to take the flag down.

With that dangerous scenario in mind, we took the only sensible decision that was available to us, we evacuated the library and cordoned off the whole area.

Now anyone who has any experience of this sort of situation will tell you, that when you make this sort of call, you are 100% certain that you are in for a long day.

Inevitably, due to the high demands made for their services, it takes 'Felix,' the army bomb disposal team some time to get to you. Then, as their work requires great caution, it would take even longer to deal with each particular incident. But, as I mentioned earlier, we simply had no other option.

Army bomb disposal vehicle

1970s Nothern Ireland Felix
Bomb disposal logo

As it happens, Felix and his team of experts were with us relatively quickly and they immediately sent a couple of guys up onto the roof area, to get a really good look at the device! While they were busy with their work, we were stuck on a cordon located near Sevastopol Street.

Our role there was to keep members of the public away from the danger area, for their safety.

As was always the case, in these situations in these areas, crowds of locals seemed to take great delight in gathering around to give those who were actually there with the sole purpose of making their area safe, dogs abuse! Whilst initially it was confined to shouting and screaming at us, it didn't take long for that to develop into throwing stones and bottles.

As the military guys were up on the roof, both my Sergeant and I were standing close to our Land Rover, which was in Sevastopol Street near to its junction with the Falls Road. A crowd of around 30 to 40 noisy and troublesome youths, had by this stage gathered a little further up the side street.

Then, from the middle of this crowd, one youth emerged and ran forward towards the side of the library. He was armed with two bottles, one in each hand. He proceeded to throw both bottles, one after the other, up toward the roof of the library, undoubtedly trying to hit the soldiers. He then disappeared back into the crowd before re-emerging with another bottle, which he then aimed and threw at us! We managed to jump out of its way as it shattered across the ground at our feet.

This incident occurred in broad daylight, my Sergeant and I were no more than 30 yards away from the offender and I was in absolutely no doubt who he was! His name was Christopher 'Crip' McWilliams, from Sevastopol Street. He was particularly easily recognised that day as he was neither hooded nor masked, and he also had flame-red hair. To perform an arrest at that time was totally impractical, so I just logged the incident and notified my Sergeant that I would deal with this matter at a more appropriate time.

Amazingly, just three hours after the first call to the Police, at around 12:30 p.m., the bomb disposal guys had done their work and were able to declare the incident an elaborate hoax. We were then able to lift our cordons and inform all those who had been affected, that the area was now safe. The library staff returned to work shortly afterwards, and things very quickly got back to normal.

Over the coming days and weeks, I kept a watchful eye out for McWilliams, intending to challenge him regarding his actions that day. Somehow or other our paths just never crossed.

However, a full five months later (just before the six-month mark, when it could have been statute barred) I received information to the effect that McWilliams would be attending Belfast Petty Sessions Court in Chichester Street, on the morning of February 5, 1981. So, I made my way to the court and waited for an opportunity to challenge him. Just as he was coming out of court, before he had exited the building onto the open street, I waylaid him. I reminded him of that day and his actions and asked if he remembered it. Needless to say, he denied all knowledge of the incident, but I went through the procedure of cautioning him and telling him that I would be reporting him to my authorities, intending to prosecute him for riotous behaviour. He made no reply after caution and actually sniggered as he walked away. Undoubtedly, he wasn't taking this matter very seriously!

I remember thinking to myself, that when we got to court, I would have the last laugh! But with hindsight I really wonder! His day in court turned into yet another opportunity for him to snub-his-nose at the legal system. Literally for months on end, on each and every occasion his case was due to be heard by the Resident Magistrate, his solicitor appeared on his behalf and asked for an adjournment, for some stupid reason or another! It seemed he just never turned up! Yet every single summons that I received, I simply had to attend! If I was on leave, leave would be cancelled! If I was on a Rest Day, the Rest Day would be cancelled! If I was on nightshift, I would even have to get up out of bed to attend!

Eventually, after months of playing the system, he pleaded guilty to a lesser charge of Disorderly Behaviour and received nothing more than a slap on the wrist. The court seemed to have allowed itself to be tied up in knots. It seemed everyone else was well aware that he was playing games and that when it came to the bit, he would just plead guilty!

The frustration of being a police Constable!

Postscript

However, little was I to know at the time of this fairly minor incident, of the infamy and notoriety that this particular individual would eventually bring upon himself.

Over the succeeding months and years, he remained a very active republican. Indeed, he went on to become one of the INLA/IPLO's most ruthless gunmen. Perhaps his most infamous act was that whilst he was serving a prison sentence for murdering a catholic bar manager, he further murdered well-known loyalist Billy Wright, within the grounds of the Maze Prison

CHAPTER 10

Watch The Person Beside You, He Could Be a Brit.

Diary Date:	February, 1980.
Incident:	Alarm Call to Public House, Falls Road.
Background:	Normal Night Shift.
Storyteller:	Andrew.

Around 10:45 p.m. on a date in February 1980 which I simply can't remember, along with the rest of my section colleagues, I paraded for night duty in Springfield Road RUC Station. Whilst shift patterns and hours changed over the years, back then a routine night shift duty entailed working from 11 p.m.–7 a.m. for seven nights in a row. That night I was detailed to carry out the duties of an extra observer in the main patrol vehicle Bravo Delta Eight Zero. At our pre-duty briefing, we were informed that our section Inspector, radio call-sign Bravo Delta Six, would be accompanying us for the duration of our shift. His presence brought our vehicle crew up to five police officers that night.

Quite early on in the shift, sometime around 1 a.m., we received a report from our radio control room to the effect that an audible burglar alarm had just been activated at one of the public houses in our area. This particular bar was located on the main Falls Road, just below the traffic lights at the junction of the Springfield and Grosvenor Roads, so we very quickly responded by taking our patrol vehicle down past the bar to check it out. From the front, as there was no access to the rear of the premises, besides the sound of the audible alarm there were no obvious signs of damage or forced entry to the building. Our Inspector reported this to our control room and asked if they would make contact with the listed key holder for the premises and ask them to come down and check the security of the building. He further mentioned that if the key holder would give us an estimated time of arrival, we would meet him at the bar just as an extra bit of security for his welfare.

Our radio controller eventually replied to us stating that he had made contact with the key holder but that it would be over an hour before he could attend to his premises, as he lived outside Belfast. After acknowledging this message, we continued with our patrol. Within the space of an hour, we received an update on the alarm call, informing us that the key holder had arrived at the premises and that he would like us to be on hand just in case someone had gained access to his premises from the rear.

When we arrived back, the key holder stepped out of his parked car and most unusually for that time, approached our Inspector with a smile on his face and greeted him with a handshake! He then made his way up to the front door, opened it and stood back allowing us to go in ahead of him. We carried out a full check around the inside of the building, which was enough to confirm that nothing sinister had activated the alarm and that all was as it should be.

I intimated to this reality earlier in my story, but I do believe it bears repeating in what is perhaps a more forthright manner. As a serving policeman in Springfield Road at that time, to be greeted by anyone in that area with anything other than a scowl or a foul mouth tirade, was honestly considered most unusual! Therefore, meeting up with and being able to perform what was a very basic police task for this appreciative businessman, was a very rare and gratifying experience for all of us that day. He expressed that he would really like each of us to have a 'wee drink' on the house, as an expression of his gratitude to us. So, purely for the betterment of Community Relations and not wanting to offend this gentleman by refusing him, we 'reluctantly' took up this most generous offer. I remember quite well our Inspector standing at the end of the bar enjoying a glass of beer, as he chatted with the bar owner. I'm sure our Community Relations branch would have been very pleased with our 'sacrificial efforts' that night!

Now perhaps this was one of those moments that you really had to be there or to witness first-hand to fully appreciate, but honestly the total paradox of that night's happenings in that Falls Road Bar, I believe warrants a retelling.

Consider if you will, this image!

Five heavily armed and fully kitted out RUC men relaxing inside this bar, which of course was and remains to this day, deep in the very heartland of Republican west Belfast! Whilst enjoying our quiet tipple a couple of us had placed our Sterling Machine Guns and M1 rifles up on top of the bar, setting them beside our pint glasses. Most bizarre!

To this day I retain a really surreal but very fond image of one of my very dear colleagues who sadly is no longer with us. We were beside each other chatting, and like the rest of our crew he was totally laden down with his flak jacket and full kit. In my minds-eye I can still see him with his M1 carbine rifle seemingly very casually slung over his right shoulder, and he was also holding a pint tumbler in that hand. At that precise moment his police cap seemed to be sitting way back on his head and it was precariously balancing there at a really silly angle. As ever, he was acting 'the eejit,' at which he was an expert!

By this stage I had actually pulled up a comfortable bar stool and was sitting on it. Whilst still standing, he was kinda leaning against what I seem to remember was a red brick supporting pillar which obviously ran from the floor to the ceiling. The pillar was covered in community notices and pro-republican posters, one of which just happened to be right above his head. I remember it issued this warning to anyone who cared to read it.

'Watch The Person Beside You, He Could Be A Brit!'
'Loose Talk Costs Lives!'

As I said there were numerous pro-republican and anti-Brit posters there and by the miracle of modern technology, I have managed to locate a copy of one of those posters which I remember were 'decorating' the pillar. See below.

Anti-Brit poster

The irony of our situation wasn't lost on us, as we each took the time to enjoy what in all honesty was a very rare moment of quiet reflection!

You really couldn't make this up! It was a totally bizarre experience!

Postscript

This was a real one-off experience, nothing remotely like this ever happened again in all of my 25 years of police service.

CHAPTER 11

Bravo Delta Eight Zero High and Dry!

Diary Date:	April 7, 1980.
Incident:	Land Rover Isolated and Engulfed by Rioters.
Background:	Normal Late Shift.
Storyteller:	Colin.

On Monday evening April 7, 1980, I was the extra observer in the rear of a single vehicle RUC Land Rover patrol, working out of Springfield Road. Around 8 p.m. and whilst on general patrol, we were made aware by radio from our control room, that a large crowd of youths were gathering and causing traffic disruption on the Falls Road, near to Dunville Park. I remember that earlier that day an Easter Rising Commemoration Rally had been held at Milltown Cemetery and it seemed tensions within the area remained high.

The area of the call is basically at the main intersection of the Falls Road, Springfield Road and Grosvenor Road. A really busy junction, meaning that this was a call which would need our prompt attention. We drove down the Falls Road and approached the junction whilst travelling in a citywards direction, allowing us a good view of the junction for some 100 to 200 meters.

Even from that distance, we could see that the main thoroughfare of the Falls Road, was at that particular point heavily littered with what seemed to be the debris of a riot. Broken glass, rocks, milk crates etc. were strewn across the main road. This was not an uncommon situation for this particular area at that time, so we felt fairly comfortable to continue our patrol.

It was only when we had fully committed through the junction, just beyond the two readily available escape routes, which were the Springfield Road and the Grosvenor Road, that a large crowd of rioters re-emerged from Dunville Park on our right, and the Clonard area on our left. A hail of bricks and bottles then battered our Land Rover, causing us to slow down. Then, just as we were at the Falls Road junction with McQuillan Street, a beer keg was rolled across our path. Whether aimed or not, it eventually rolled beneath the front of our vehicle, forcing us to come to a shuddering halt!

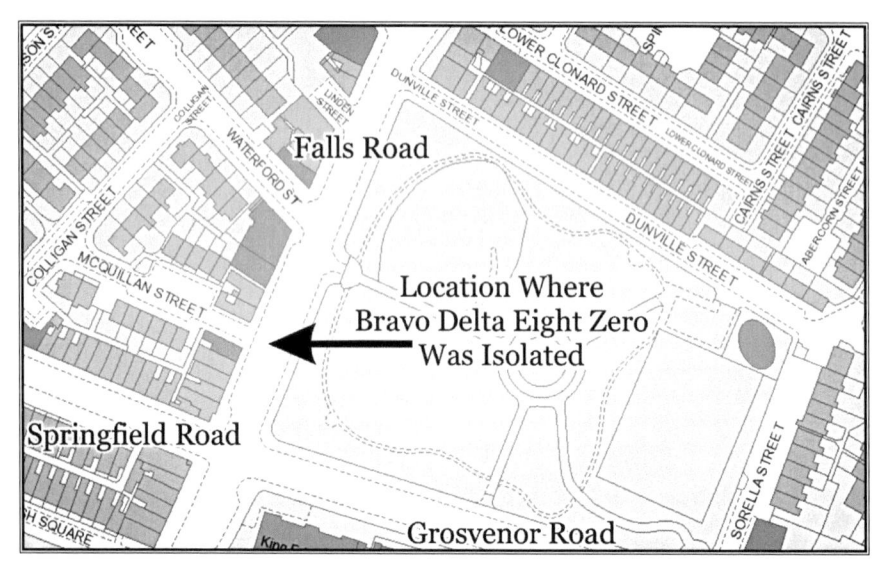

Bravo Eight Zero Isolated

With the beer keg now seemingly wedged below our vehicle ensuring that we couldn't move, we were then literally engulfed by what seemed to be hundreds of rioters. They surged forward in huge numbers, totally surrounding us. There was nothing we could do, as the crowd swarmed all over our vehicle. Our heavily armoured, long-wheelbase Land Rover, which is a really weighty vehicle was being rocked side to side by the angry crowd. They were also trying their best to open the vehicle's doors, to get inside to us!

I was alone in the back of the Rover, trying grimly to hold the handle of the vehicle's double doors in the shut position. I can vividly recall looking out through the two small, armoured windows of the back doors, as the crowd frantically hammered and bashed at the door's outer handles. Realising that they weren't physically going to be able to force the doors open, they tried hammering the external door handles with breeze blocks.

Then, as they were becoming increasingly frustrated by their inability to force open the back doors, from nowhere they managed to produce yet another beer-keg. It was put to use as an even heavier hammer, as they continued to bash away at the handles. Each strike on the outside sent shockwaves shuddering up my arms, as I desperately clung to the inside handle.

As the crowd were no more than 10-12 inches from me, only being separated by those two small squares of armoured glass, I had a remarkably close encounter with this snarling mob! I knew they wanted nothing more than to get their hands on me! I could see their anger and their hatred of us was almost tangible! I remember wondering just how long I would be able to keep them at bay! I was in no doubt that if they had gained access to the vehicle, they would have torn us limb from limb!

Then, somehow or other, perhaps brought about by the crazed crowd rocking our vehicle, the beer keg eventually worked itself loose. We were then able to cautiously drive out of the immediate danger, where we had been for what seemed to be an eternity, but in reality, was probably no more than five minutes.

Springfield Road Hotspur without front or side skirts, sitting outside Springfield Road Station.

CHAPTER 12

Bravo Delta Eight Zero Stranded in Divis Complex!

Diary Date:	June 1980.
Incident:	Land Rover Stranded in St. Peter's.
Background:	Normal Late Shift.
Storyteller:	Jimmy.

This story relates to an incident in which I was involved, which occurred in early June 1980. I'm not able to be any more definitive about the actual date, but I do know it happened whilst we were on a Late turn of duty, 3 p.m.-11 p.m. Our section had paraded for duty as normal, where our Sergeant detailed the duties for the evening that lay ahead. I was detailed to be the driver of Bravo Delta Eight Zero, the main District Mobile Patrol vehicle, which that night had a crew of four members in total.

The early period of our shift had been quite uneventful, so when at around 9 p.m. that evening, we received a call to assist our colleagues in Hasting Street station, we were more than happy to head down to see how we could be of assistance. On entering through the big security gates, I continued to drive down through the old open station yard area towards the front door of the actual station, which was on our left.

As we neared the station, I did notice that their patrol vehicle, Bravo Hotel Eight Zero, was parked just outside the front door. However, it was only when we got out of our vehicle and were walking toward the station that we noticed the front passenger's side and windscreen of their Land Rover, were covered in paint. I should point out that this wasn't what you might call an altogether rare occurrence back then, as quite frankly police vehicles were daily targets for all sorts of missiles, which included paint bombs.

What was notable though, was the most unusual colour of the paint which was still dripping off the vehicle. The colour was probably best described as being a strong shade of peppermint green!

As our crew traipsed into the station enquiry office, we were all discussing and joking about the accuracy of the paint bomb 'strike' on the vehicle. Hastings Street was one of those really quaint old-school stations. Throughout the 'barracks' the rooms and office areas were what nowadays you might describe as being 'intimate,' but in reality, they were just small! The only source of heat in the enquiry office came from a closed-in glass stove, which more often than not, seemed to be lit.

Anyway, when we got inside, the sight which met our eyes was something to behold! The Hastings Street section Sergeant, who although being quite diminutive in stature, was a vastly experienced, capable and very popular officer, had been part of the crew at the time of the paint bomb strike. His startling appearance at that particular point, rather belied those capabilities and unquestionably told all of us that on that particular occasion, he had made what can only be described as a 'beginners' error!

The 'Cosy' Guard Room, at Hastings Street RUC Station
Painting by Desmond (Desi) Dobbin
Murdered October 11, 1986.
Permission Granted

I'll explain!

Earlier that evening the Hastings Street mobile patrol, Bravo Hotel Eight Zero, had been pursuing a stolen car, a Ford Escort RS2000, through the Albert Street/Divis Flats area. During that pursuit they had at one point stopped their vehicle convenient to one of the lower tower-blocks. I have no definitive reason as to why they did this, but I imagine part of the thinking behind this action was that if they stopped their vehicle temporarily, they could turn off the engine and then by opening one of the doors they just might be able to hear what direction the stolen car was coming from. For whatever reason, that's exactly what the Sergeant did!

This action was a Mistake. No, sorry, it wasn't just a mistake, it was a really, really BIG MISTAKE!

As you're probably already aware, a static police vehicle with at least one of the doors ajar in Divis flats, created a perfect target and a wonderful opportunity for anyone who at that time just happened to be maliciously loitering about on one of the upper levels of the flats. Additionally, at that very moment, he would also just happen to have had access to a ready supply of bricks, bottles or perhaps even a peppermint-coloured paint bomb to launch at the police. Recognising this opportune moment and undoubtedly with well-practised precision, the 'paint bomber' then launched his 'peppermint green paint bomb,' from one of the flat's upper levels. From his perspective, his delivery was perfect! He scored a direct hit on the police vehicle, striking at the high point above the open passenger side door. The result was that most of the paint cascaded into the police vehicle and all over the front seat passenger, who just happened to be the aforementioned Sergeant.

Now standing barefoot beside the fire, the Sergeant was looking rather sheepish and undoubtedly feeling somewhat sorry for himself. His appearance bore testimony to the accuracy of the paint bomb strike! His left-hand side had been completely saturated in paint! Bizarrely though, his appearance would I'm sure be considered as a perfect example of a split personality! As in contrast the right-hand side of his body, trousers, tunic, his head and face were seemingly untouched. However, the left-hand side, where the paint had struck, literally appeared to be a peppermint green-coloured, mirror image of his right-hand side!

Initially we were all dumbstruck! In truth, as we weren't that familiar with this particular Sergeant, we just weren't sure how he would take to a brutal 'ribbing' from a crowd of peelers whom he didn't know. Unquestionably though, his appearance more than warranted berating! We didn't know where to look or what to say! Then one of his own section members who obviously would have known him better than we did, appeared on the scene and unceremoniously pronounced, "Flip

Sarge, you look like a giant Pacer!" Thankfully the poor Sergeant saw the funny side as everyone exploded into fits of laughter!

For those who don't remember, 'Pacers' were green and white peppermint chewy sweets, which were all over the TV at that time!

One of my favourite sweets

When we all got ourselves calmed down and decided that we had given the 'Giant Pacer' more than his fair share of abuse, the Hastings Street crew eventually got round to mentioning why they had called us down to their station in the first place! As their patrol vehicle was temporarily off the road, they asked us if we would take a run up through the Albert Street/Divis area, to see could we locate the stolen RS2000, as it had been reported to be still in that area.

We made our way out of the station and headed up the Falls Road before making a left-hand turn into Albert Street. We weren't there very long, when with its lights flashing and horn blasting, the stolen RS2000 made its grand entrance just in front of our vehicle. Being well aware of that particular Ford Escorts capabilities we were really in no position to pursue it in any meaningful manner, however as it careered past us heading up towards the Falls, I decided that I would perform a three-point turn in our vehicle and head back in that general direction.

Rather than drive about that particular area with our Land Rover lights on, and thus advertise our presence, I decided that I would turn them off temporarily whilst I performed this particularly slow manoeuvre. The last thing which we wanted to do was attract any unwelcome attention from the locals to our presence, in what was a notably hostile and dangerous area for police.

I swung the Land Rover into what I at that time thought was a dark recessed part of the roadway, but I suddenly realised that it wasn't part of the road at all, it was actually a set of really large and unlit steps which led down into the grounds of Saint Peter's Chapel. Unfortunately, these particular steps were of a height, depth and length that our Land Rovers wheel span just couldn't deal with. As a consequence, our vehicle was left high-and-dry, see-sawing back and forth with neither the front nor back wheels able to get any traction on terra firma! We were as they say, 'up the creek without a paddle!'

The reality of the situation we now found ourselves in was this. With the Hastings Street vehicle being off-the-road, our nearest police help would be from Andersonstown Station, which was around three or four miles away! Alternatively, we could ask the Army for help, which is just what we did via our control room at Springfield Road. They made the call to the nearby Army garrison of North Howard Street, to come to our rescue just as quickly as they could. That base would have been no more than half a mile away.

As we waited for help to arrive, it seemed our predicament resembled that of a wounded animal, isolated and exposed to the wilds of the jungle! Seemingly from nowhere groups of predators appeared, and with an endless supply of bricks and bottles at the ready, they began their frenzied attack on our defenceless vehicle! News of our vulnerability spread through the area like wildfire, as the crowd's numbers increased by the minute.

Then, just when we thought things couldn't get any worse, it seemed they did! As we watched helplessly from inside the vehicle, we noticed that the surrounding crowd were then setting light to any old newspapers which they could get their hands on, before approaching our vehicle and throwing them onto the ground. Initially we were kinda bemused by this, as we just couldn't figure out what they were up to.

However, we soon learned exactly what they were trying to do, when on closer inspection it became apparent that our vehicle was leaking oil and petrol from the engine area, and the crowd who had noticed this before we had, were trying to ignite the fuel spillage which was flowing from our vehicle!

I'll never forget that my observer that night was a young female probationer officer, who hadn't been with us very long and despite the fact that she was very keen and indeed really capable, she honestly was someone who at that time just wasn't used to these sorts of situations. I probably wouldn't be allowed to say this nowadays, but she was someone whom our section felt particularly protective off. Not least because at that particular juncture in the history of the RUC, policewomen were not routinely armed with personal protection weapons. Being aware of her situation and also assured in the knowledge that the two experienced extra observers in the back of the vehicle had each signed out either SMG's or M1's from the station armoury, I unholstered my personal protection Walther Pistol, flicked off the safety catch and handed the gun over to her for the duration of the incident.

It's amazing the way some quite seemingly unimportant things stand out in your memory, and this is one of them. In the midst of all the hustle and bustle and the noise of bricks thumping off our Land Rover, I remember thinking; flip I can hear someone's voice quite distinctly over all that hullabaloo! I was aware that this voice was coming from a position to my right and from slightly behind me, so I very carefully nudged open my driver's door just enough to let me see if I could identify whose voice I was hearing. Lo and behold, there at the forefront of the crowd, standing between them and our marooned vehicle was the Parish Priest, Father Newberry. He was talking to the crowd, seemingly trying to reason with them and I clearly heard him urging them to make their way home. He had some level of success, as the frenzied crowd undoubtedly seemed to calm down a bit at his behest.

Very soon after the greatly appreciated intervention by the Parish Priest, we all heard the easily identifiable and ever-so-welcome noise of an approaching Army Pig. No sooner had they arrived at the scene when two soldiers dismounted from the rear doors and ran towards the front of our Land Rover. They proceeded to wrap what was a very heavy set of tow chains around the front of the vehicle, before attaching the other end to the back of their Pig. Once everyone was safely aboard, the Army very slowly but surely towed us out of that immediate danger zone and returned us back to the safety of our home station Springfield Road.

Postscript

Unfortunately, in recovering our vehicle from St Peter's that night, somehow our engine sump must have become dislodged or cracked, as we left behind an awful oily mess on the Chapel steps.

CHAPTER 13

IRA Terrorist Shot Dead Whilst on Active Service.

Diary Date:	July 1, 1980.
Incident:	Whiterock Road Shooting.
Background:	Normal Late Shift.
Storyteller:	George.

On the evening of Tuesday July 1, 1980, I was part of a three-man RUC Land Rover patrol which was on general duty in the Springfield Road area of West Belfast. At around 9:30pm, our vehicle turned off the Falls Road and began driving up the Whiterock Road. With the perimeter wall of the City Cemetery on our left, we steadily made our way country-wards towards the Whiterock junction with Springfield Road, an area known locally as Kelly's Corner.

However, when we were approximately two to three hundred yards short of Kelly's, two hooded figures suddenly emerged from a small side road on our left. Running across the road immediately in front of our vehicle, they didn't initially seem to notice that the vehicle approaching them was actually a police Hotspur. When that reality struck home, one of the pair raised a handgun and began firing at us. Our driver literally stood on the brakes, bringing our vehicle to a shuddering halt just as quickly as was humanly possible. Jumping out, we shouted verbal warnings that we were armed police. Ignoring our warnings, the gunman continued to fire at us as the pair bolted across the footpath. They darted into a small, paved laneway, which leads from the Whiterock Road into Glenalina Crescent.

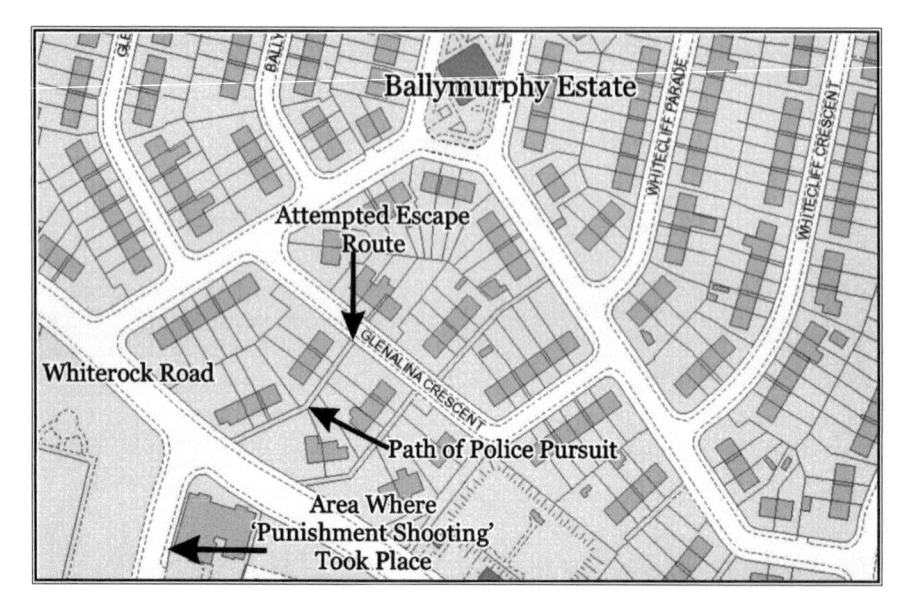

The Escape Route

Returning fire, we continued to chase the fleeing pair into the lane. Just short of Glenalina Crescent, we came across one of those whom we had been pursuing. He was lying prostrate on the ground and was bleeding from what seemed to be a single fresh gunshot wound to his chest.

We immediately provided first-aid, but due to the location of this incident (Ballymurphy Estate) and the prevailing danger that being there presented to us, we felt it would be best to carry the injured man back to our vehicle and continue with our first aid in the safety of the Land Rover. It very quickly became clear that the gunshot wound was serious. So rather than radio for assistance and then have to wait for the arrival of an ambulance, we loaded the injured man into the back of the vehicle and made our way directly to the casualty department of the nearby Royal Victoria Hospital.

Immediately on our arrival, the wounded man was promptly taken into the casualty area where he was treated by the medical staff. A short time later one of the doctors who had been attending the casualty, came out and informed us that the injured man had died. He went on to say that whilst treating him, a member of the nursing staff had found a gun in the deceased man's pocket, which he then handed over to us.

Postscript

The full story behind the basic facts of this incident became clearer over the following days, as not only did the police carry out a full and thorough investigation into the matter, but the local news media also gave it considerable column inches.

The deceased man was identified as being 26-year-old Terence 'Teddy' O'Neill, from Glenalina Road in Ballymurphy. Through recognised media outlets the IRA claimed that he had been a member of their organisation, elaborating that at the time of his death, he had been on 'IRA active service.' The 'active service' that O'Neill had been involved in that evening soon became apparent. A fifteen-year-old youth was found with a gunshot wound to one of his legs at the rear of the Whiterock Community Centre, in Whiterock Close. The precise reason behind this particular 'punishment shooting' is unknown, but such actions were often carried out by various paramilitary groupings as punishments, for what they deemed to be anti-social behaviour by the victim. The area where this 'punishment shooting' took place was of course the precise area from which the two hooded men had been fleeing, when they encountered our police patrol.

Approximately three hours after the police shooting at the Whiterock Road, three armed men hijacked a car on the Monagh Road. That car was recovered the following day in nearby Ardmonagh Gardens, with Police noting at the time of its recovery that the back seat was saturated with blood.

Whilst never able to prove or disprove their suspicions, those investigating this occurrence believed that both incidents were related. The inference was that the second man who had been with O'Neill, had also sustained gunshot wounds. Somehow, he had managed to evade the chasing police before 'going to ground' in the local vicinity, where he would have received a friendly welcome!

The car hijacking would undoubtedly have been at the behest of the local IRA, thus providing them with transport to move their injured man out of the immediate vicinity. He would then have been taken to a different location, where he would undoubtedly have received private medical treatment. This rather convoluted course of action would have allowed them to overcome the potential problem of taking him to a mainstream hospital, which would then have brought the nature of their man's injuries, to the attention of the police.

Inquest

Almost a year after the actual incident, in April 1981, the Belfast City Coroner held an inquest to examine the circumstances which led to the death of Terence O'Neill that night in July 1980. His findings, according to the detail's published by the local press, determined that O'Neill had been shot after he had refused to stop, on being challenged to do so by the Police.

A verdict, that was in accordance with the unquestionable medical evidence, was eventually issued.

Over the duration of the Inquest, the coroner heard and accepted evidence which ultimately reinforced the narrative that O'Neill and a still to be identified unknown companion, who were both masked, had ran across the front of the Police vehicle whilst it was travelling up the Whiterock Road. The Police officers had stopped their vehicle, dismounted and verbally challenged the two fleeing figures to stop. Both continued running, but one of the two turned and shot at the Police using a handgun, before the Police returned fire. Continuing the chase on foot, the Police very quickly located one of those they had been pursuing (later identified as O'Neill) lying on the ground with a gunshot wound to his chest.

The court heard that contrary to what the Police believed at the time, O'Neill was actually dead by the time he had been transported to the Royal Victoria Hospital. Testimony was given to the court by firearm forensic experts to the effect that the gun which had been recovered from O'Neill's person, had previously been used in one murder, an attempted murder and a further eight so called 'punishment shootings.'

In the form of a written statement the unfortunate youth who had been 'kneecapped' that night, gave his testimony to the court. He recounted that after being in the centre for around ten minutes, (Whiterock Community Centre) he had been accosted by two men. Brandishing a gun, they ordered him to come outside with them. Then, despite his protestations that he had done nothing wrong, they pushed him against a wall and shot him once in the leg.

Additional Relevant Information

The National Graves Association, which was founded in Dublin in 1921, are an organisation which has as its raison d'être: - the maintenance of the graves, the recording of the deaths and the fostering of respect for all those they believe who have died for Irish Freedom.

In 1985 this particular association brought out a paperback book entitled 'Belfast Graves,' in which they have compiled 'pen-portraits,' of many of whom they believe have such a claim. Terence O'Neill is one of those whose name and story is included. Unsurprisingly, the description recorded therein is significantly different to that which was given by the Police and later accepted by the coroner.

"On July 1, 1980, near the Ballymurphy Tenants Association on the Whiterock Road, Vol. Teddy O'Neill made the ultimate sacrifice for the country he loved. After carrying out a punishment shooting, he and his comrade, both wearing hoods, were spotted by an RUC mobile patrol. Teddy had concealed his pistol, and his comrade was unarmed. Heavily armed RUC men leapt from their vehicles and opened fire without warning, on the two Volunteers. Teddy was hit and fell seriously wounded. His comrade escaped the indiscriminate fusillade of bullets.

As Teddy lay on the ground, bleeding profusely, an RUC man ran up to him and pumped several rifle shots into his body. He was then dragged along the ground for about 30 yards and thrown into the back of an RUC Land Rover."

CHAPTER 14

Attempted Murder at RPG Avenue.

Diary Date:	May 13, 1981.
Incident:	Fault in RPG, Saves RUC Patrol.
Background:	12 Hour Shifts for Hunger Strike.
Storyteller:	Andrew, George.

Background to Incident

On March 1, 1981, convicted IRA terrorist Bobby Sands became the first of a series of republican prisoners to commence a hunger strike in the Maze Prison. Hunger Strikes were a tactic which had been well-used throughout the history of the republican movement, dating back at least as far as the 1916-1923 revolutionary period. Accompanying them with a systematic upscaling of their vicious terrorist campaign, an escalation of widespread street disorder and ever-increasing political pressure by their representatives, the hunger strikers sought to coerce the government of the day to award them 'special category status.' Their belief was that as their crimes were politically motivated, they should not be viewed as ordinary criminals.

The United Kingdom Conservative Government of that time did not share those beliefs. Indeed, Tory Prime Minister Margaret Thatcher made her thoughts on this precise matter very clear when she said, "Crime is crime is crime" she declared. "It is not political. It is crime. There can be no question of political status."

Some 66 days into his hunger strike, Sands died on May 5, 1981. Seven days later, another IRA prisoner, Francis Hughes died, and over the following three months, a further eight hunger strikers took their own lives.

Many security force experts of the day, believed that the huge level of street disorder and violence that the country had experienced in the lead-up to the actual first deaths of the hunger strikers, could neither be sustained nor raised. Unfortunately, their assessment of this situation was way out!

Following the deaths of each succeeding Hunger Striker, just about every republican area in the country, saw widespread street disorder and violence, on a scale like never seen before or since! These areas came to a virtual standstill, with many thousands of residents taking to the streets in protest.

To maintain a semblance of law and order, the RUC assisted by their colleagues in the Army, were stretched to breaking point! Across the country, police personnel were put on permanent 12-hour shifts, which allowed stations like Springfield Road to 'double-up' their patrol capacity. There was nowhere within these areas that police weren't daily, under the threat of attack by brick, petrol-bomb, bullet or even rocket!

The area had seemingly become a war zone.

Two separate members from that night's crew of Bravo Delta Eight Zero, the Driver and one of the two Extra Observers, here share their personal memories of that night's incident.

The Driver

At around 8 p.m. on the evening of Wednesday May 13, 1981, I was the driver of the lead call-sign of what was a two-vehicle mobile patrol, Bravo Delta Eight Zero and Bravo Delta Eight One. At that time, we were on general patrol and were travelling citywards on the Falls Road. Our vehicle-crew was made up of two constables, acting as extra observers in the rear of the vehicle, and our section sergeant was in the front passenger seat.

On passing the top of the Donegal Road, our patrol vehicle steadily rounded a right-hand bend on the main Falls, convenient to its junction with La Salle Drive which was also on our right. Once round that bend, the main road opens up and straightens out considerably, meaning I had an unobstructed view citywards for approximately 300-400 metres. It very soon became clear that there was a huge crowd of rioters milling around the road and blocking the free passage of traffic on the main Falls Road, near to its junction with Beechmount Avenue which was on our left-hand side.

As we approached this crowd, I slowed our vehicle down a bit, to enable me to assess what was actually happening. It soon became apparent that not only had we seen the crowd, but that the crowd had also seen us, as they started to disperse into the side streets around the junction. By the time we had got to within approximately 50 metres from the Beechmount Avenue junction, the huge crowd had virtually disappeared off the main road.

I can then remember seeing a man running out of the Beechmount Avenue junction. He was running across the main road, from our left-hand side to our right. There was nothing distinctive about this person, other than he was dragging a rope behind him. It seems to be taking an age to tell this story, but in actuality it was over in seconds!

When this unknown person, whose face and head I seem to remember were covered by a mask or balaclava, reached the footpath on the right-hand side of the road, he immediately spun round to face the direction from which he had come. Then, using both hands, he rapidly started pulling the rope which he had been carrying, towards him.

By this stage I would say we were within 20 or 30 meters from him. I had slowed our vehicle way down, placing it in a low gear in an effort to make what in truth was a very heavy and sluggish vehicle, just a little bit more responsive.

It was then that I noticed that the rope this man was dragging across the road, was actually attached to a series of 7 or 8 heavy beer kegs. Undoubtedly, he was trying to drag these beer kegs across the road in an effort to block our passage. My immediate reaction was to accelerate our vehicle just as hard as it would go, whilst steering it directly at the guy pulling the rope.

When he realised that our '3 Ton' vehicle was heading straight for him, he immediately dropped the rope and fled. I then drove our vehicle up and onto the footpath, thus avoiding the beer-kegs which were then spread out across the main road, before accelerating away down the pavement in a citywards direction.

However, just as he turned tail, and before we could fully extricate ourselves out of the immediate area, our vehicles came under a heavy and sustained gun attack. Both of our vehicles were struck numerous times by the gunfire. We could literally hear the gunfire and then the noise of the bullets 'pinging' of the side plating of our armoured Hotspur. Thankfully we were able to ride-out the attack and both vehicles made our way back to the safety of our home station, which was just a few minutes away. On our safe arrival we nervously took stock of what had just happened. Counting the strike marks on our vehicles, we joked and laughed about the incident. In truth it was only by having such a really dark sense of humour, that we got through what were unbelievably dangerous times to be a member of the police in Northern Ireland.

This attempted ambush had been meticulously planned and well thought out. They believed that by blocking the main road with beer kegs, it would ensure our vehicles would have to stop and therefore become sitting ducks!

At a briefing, some days after this attack we were informed by members of our Special Branch department, just how this particular terrorist plan was supposed to have played out. Once the patrol vehicles had been stopped or preferably totally immobilised by the line of beer-kegs, terrorists would then have stepped out from the safety of their hideouts in Beechmount Avenue, before launching an RPG7 rocket at us. That attack would then have been followed up by an onslaught of gunfire.

The location of this incident was as I mentioned previously, Beechmount Avenue. To this very day that particular thoroughfare carries the colloquial street name of 'RPG AVENUE.'

Beechmount Avenue, aka RPG Avenue

The Extra Observer

On the evening of May 13, 1981, I was one of two extra observers in the Springfield Road mobile patrol vehicle Bravo Delta Eight Zero, travelling citywards on the Falls Road. My colleague's account regarding this incident, which was written from the driver's perspective, whilst a bit more detailed than what I could personally testify to, was just how I remember that night. However, my experience which is of being in the back of our armour-plated Land Rover, is as a consequence unsurprisingly different from his, and as such bears retelling.

Our personal accounts of this particular incident, differ due to the very different roles we had in that night's vehicle crew. Unlike the clear and unobstructed view enjoyed by both our driver and front seat passenger, my view from the back of a Land Rover was much more restricted. As we approached Beechmount Avenue I was aware that our vehicle was slowing down, but at that point, without changing my body position I couldn't have told why we were slowing. Consequently, by turning my body toward the front of our vehicle and by lowering my head, into what admittedly was quite an uncomfortable position, I was then able to get a bit of a look through the front windscreen of our vehicle.

We were still a couple of hundred yards short of that junction, but I do remember seeing that the main road was heavily congested with rioters. As a consequence, I loaded up my Federal Riot Gun (plastic bullet gun) and just in case our vehicle was attacked by the rioters, I opened one of the two firing hatches on its near side.

As we got ever closer to the main junction, I was alternating my viewing position. Initially ducking down to look out through our vehicles front windscreen, then sitting back up which allowed me to see out through the small firing hatch on the side of our vehicle. Just as we reached the junction, I was looking out the hatch which gave me a clear and unobstructed view of the footpath on that side of the road.

Two Baton Guns Showing Out the Nearside of an RUC Hotspur Land Rover

There was no mistaking what I then witnessed! Standing on the footpath, just on the city side of Beechmount Avenue and no further than 25 yards away from me, was a hooded gunman. He was holding a handgun of some sort and was in a firing stance. I can still vividly remember seeing the muzzle flash from his gun, as he blazed away at our passing vehicles.

I quickly slammed the side slot shut and listened as we came under a fairly intense gun attack. It soon became evident that the lone gunman whom I saw, had subsequently been joined by others as the amount of gunfire I heard and the number of strikes on our vehicle, simply could not have been caused by one shooter with a handgun. I also remember that as our vehicle mounted the kerb and accelerated away from the attack, I was thrown about the back of the Land Rover quite a bit!

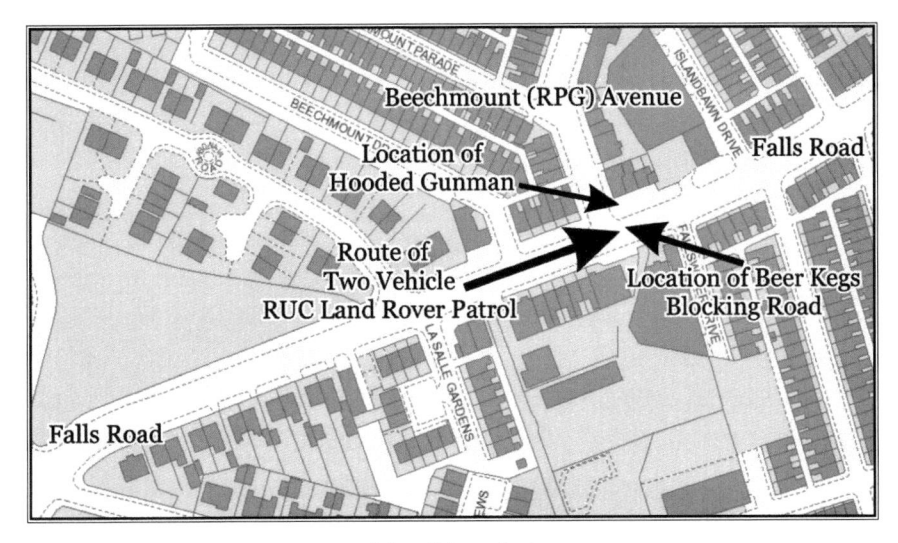

Map of the ambush

On our safe arrival back at Springfield Road and from listening to the story as retold by both our driver and observer, we all agreed that we had been very lucky to have escaped totally unscathed. The attack had been a very determined and well thought out effort to get our vehicle stopped, in what would have been a very dangerous location.

Indeed, with the benefit of hindsight we now know that the terrorists plan for that attack was to get our vehicle stopped, and then to launch an RPG attack on the static and vulnerable target. It seems that luck was on our side, as recently uncovered documents appear to reveal that an attempt to fire an RPG at us did indeed take place that night. However, that attempted murder of Police Officers was ultimately frustrated, when the rocket launcher malfunctioned. Sadly, the following night after repairs had been made to the RPG, the terrorists were eventually successful in their murderous plot!

Postscript

'Ballymurphy and the Irish War,' is a book written by Ciaran de Baroid and was first published in 1991, then re-issued with additional content in 2000. Besides documenting the growth and development of the Ballymurphy estate and its residents, it goes on to give a rare, albeit superficial glimpse at many of the activities carried out by the Active Service Units of the Ballymurphy IRA.

Without documenting the precise location, he relates how on May 13, 1981, the Ballymurphy ASU had 'set up a rocket attack for an RUC mobile patrol.' However, due to some sort of mechanical issue, the rocket failed to fire. Continuing, he goes on to say that the following night having made a homemade repair to the launcher, the same unit were successful in attacking a police patrol on the Upper Springfield Road, near to Divismore Crescent.

Unless some new additional information becomes available, which could reveal the precise location of the failed rocket attempt, it can't definitively be determined that the story of this botched ambush relates to our vehicle's incident at Beechmount Avenue. However, the similarities would most definitely suggest that they are one and the same.

Additional Relevant Information

Some nights prior to the above occurrence, a Land Rover which was working out of Hasting Street RUC Station, had actually got a beer-keg wedged directly below their vehicle. They had been travelling countrywards on the Falls Road, when near to its junction with Leeson Street they had been attacked by a group of rioters. Among the hail of petrol bombs and bricks thrown from the crowd, one of them had flung or rolled a beer-keg out into the path of the vehicle. The driver of the Land Rover found himself unable to take any evasive action and had no option but to try to drive over the heavily enforced metal keg.

Unfortunately, the keg was like a wedge, getting jammed below the vehicle and acting similarly to the pivot of a seesaw. With the keg now trapped below the vehicle, it had effectively been rendered immobile and thus became a sitting duck! Thankfully there was a heavy-duty army Saracen nearby, and it was very quickly in attendance. Despite being attacked by an ever-growing crowd of rioters who seemed to have sensed a rare opportunity to inflict serious damage on what was a vulnerable target, the army 'pig' was able to give the police vehicle a hefty nudge from the back, which was enough to get it mobile again.

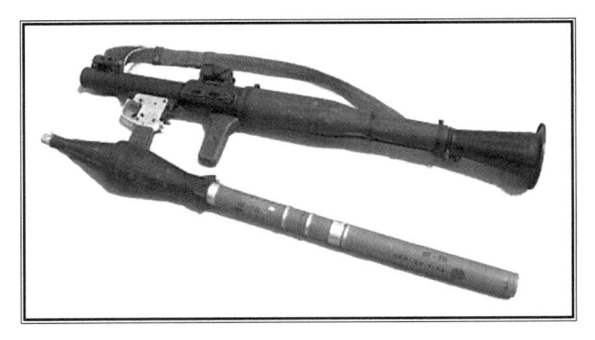

A rocket-propelled grenade and RPG-7 launcher.
The thinner cylinder is inserted into the muzzle of the launcher.

Outcome

From the first-hand experiences of Police Officers working on the front line, such as those spoken about in the above incidents, it became evident to those involved in the forces management team that there was one particular area of vulnerability in the armour of the RUC Land Rovers. That vulnerable area was of course the totally unprotected space, beneath the vehicles!

To counter this threat, our authorities came up with the idea of fitting each Police Land Rover with both front and side metal grills/skirts. This action basically put an end to what was becoming an ever-increasing problem, of rioters trying to roll beer kegs into the path of the vehicles.

CHAPTER 15

The Ultimate Sacrifice.

Diary Date:	May 14, 1981.
Incident:	Murder of Constable Sam Vallely.
Background:	12 Hour Shifts for Hunger Strike.
Storyteller:	Andrew.

Constable Samuel (Sam) Vallely, age 23. Murdered by terrorists May 14, 1981

At a pre-duty briefing on the evening of Thursday, May 14, 1981, I paraded for duty in Springfield Road Station. As this was during the IRA Hunger Strike campaign, our normal patrol shift, 'D' Section, was enhanced by colleagues from 'A' Section. This increase in personnel, enabled our authorities to deploy four mobile patrol vehicles: Bravo Delta Eight Zero, Eight One, Eight Two and Eight Three. I was detailed to be the driver of Bravo Delta Eight Zero and my section Inspector would be in charge of our crew. To increase our security, our vehicle would operate along with Bravo Delta Eight One, as a two-vehicle patrol. As such we were detailed to cover the Upper Springfield area of 'the patch.' The other two crews, Eight Two and Eight Three, again operating as a double vehicle patrol, would be responsible for the Lower Springfield and Falls Road area, under the supervision of their own 'A' section Inspector. Of course, these instructions were only guidelines, should either crew at any time require assistance, the other vehicles were only a radio message and a few minutes away.

My memory of certain parts of that night's events remains quite vivid, even though it was over 40 years ago now. Having said that, for some reason that has long since been forgotten, I seem to recall that our two-vehicle patrol, call signs Bravo Delta Eight Zero and Eight One, commenced our patrol that night by leaving the heavily fortified Springfield Road station complex by the front gates. This was not the common practice back then, as the station operated on a 'drive-through' one-way system. Vehicles routinely entered the station via the front gate and exited it by the back! Anyway, for whatever reason we exited via the 'In' gate, and I remember our Inspector telling me to turn right, citywards on the Springfield Road towards its junction with the Falls Road and Grosvenor Road. We got to that junction and again turned right, to head country-wards on the Falls Road.

Unusually for the time, the area appeared to be quite quiet. We continued travelling country-wards on the Falls Road before turning right onto the Whiterock Road, which would take us uphill towards the Springfield Road. The Whiterock Road rises gradually from its junction with the Falls Road, meandering its way upwards towards its junction with Springfield Road. That junction, known locally as Kelly's Corner, was back then viewed by security force personnel as being a potential ambush point.

Having followed that aforementioned route, we then turned right to head citywards on the Springfield Road. I can still remember, my

Inspector again remarking just how quiet the area seemed. Then, using the vehicles radio, he made contact with our control room informing them that he intended to use this seemingly quiet period to take our two vehicles to the police canteen at Springfield Parade for some hot food, in case the later part of the night got busy. Having acknowledged this message, the controller was then asked to relay this information to the other two Springfield Road mobile patrol vehicles, Bravo Delta Eight Two and Eight Three. They, as per our earlier briefing, were patrolling the area of the Lower Springfield Road and Falls Road. We further requested that they pay passing attention to our patrol area, for the brief period we would be away. "Roger That," came the reply.

Our journey then took us down the Springfield Road, before turning left onto the West Circular Road and then right into Springfield Parade, where we parked up our Land Rovers intending to head into the police canteen.

Here, I simply can't remember if we had actually got into the canteen or not, before we all heard what I would describe as a very 'loud, deep, double-punching explosion or bang!' The cause of that noise was of course unknown to us at the time; however, the true horror of its source and its terrible consequences became evident to us very quickly!

When our fellow officers in 'Bravo Delta Eight Two' and 'Eight Three' were informed that our two vehicles would be 'off the air' for a short period, they gladly took on the additional responsibility of temporarily patrolling our designated 'patch.' Indeed, it seems they literally followed the route we had travelled just a few minutes earlier. Falls Road, Whiterock Road and then a right turn to travel citywards on the Springfield Road.

Somewhere around the main roads junction with Divismore Crescent, which leads into the highly republican Ballymurphy estate, their vehicle was targeted by petrol bombers, forcing it to slow down. Of course, this was in no way out of the ordinary at that time.

However, it seems that this pre-planned petrol bomb attack wasn't an end in itself. The plan was that this attack would force the police Land Rover to slow down or perhaps even stop, thereby making it an easier target for the main thrust of the terrorist's ambush, an RPG7 rocket attack! When the vehicle slowed and from a position slightly below the level of the main road, an IRA terrorist fired the rocket at the passing patrol. The deadly projectile, originally designed as a Russian anti-tank weapon, struck the police Land Rover a thunderous blow at a high point, near the rear of the vehicle. The rocket strike caused considerable damage to the roof of the Hotspur, showering its inside with molten shrapnel. Heroically, the police driver had the presence of mind to keep driving. Despite his vehicle being badly damaged he was able to drive directly to the Casualty Department of the nearby Royal Victoria Hospital, where he and his colleagues could be treated for their injuries. Regrettably one of the vehicles passengers, 23 years old Constable Samuel Vallely, who had been sitting in the rear of the vehicle, suffered fatal injuries as a result of this attack.

Within minutes and supported by large numbers of military personnel from the nearby New Barnsley RUC/Military base, we made our way back to the scene of the RPG attack. That scene remains vivid!

On passing that precise point, just 5 or 10 minutes earlier when it had been unusually quiet, the scene now was dramatically different! We were met with a cacophony of noise from the gangs of youths now out in large numbers. The police were being attacked by stone throwers who were shouting and singing noisily, seemingly celebrating the earlier attack on the police vehicle!

Eventually members of the CID attended the scene, as they set about commencing an investigation into what would be a murder enquiry. Their immediate investigations were cut short however! Information was received that the IRA were in a position to launch further attacks on the police and military, who were currently at the scene and involved in the follow up operation.

So, whilst under the dazzling light of a military helicopters 'night sun,' it appeared that no sooner had the examination of the scene got underway, than it had to be lifted due to what we were later informed was a viable threat.

The Land Rover that Constable Samuel Vallely was travelling in.

Postscript

Just a week after Constable Vallely's funeral, whilst searching a Lada car they had forced to a stop on the Falls Road, the RUC located and recovered an RPG rocket launcher, an armed warhead, a pistol, an Armalite rifle, 100 armour piercing rounds and various other articles of terrorist equipment. The car, with two people on board, had earlier failed to stop at a police vehicle check point. When the police had managed to bring the suspect vehicle to a stop, one of those on board made an attempt to escape arrest by running away. Members of the police patrol initially gave chase, but when the suspect repeatedly failed to respond to numerous shouted warnings, an RUC officer opened fire.

The suspect was then apprehended and taken directly to the nearby Royal Victoria Hospital.

Back at the scene of the initial police stop, a large hostile crowd had gathered, some of whom attempted to 'trap' the police in situ, by placing parked cars across the main road. Those police who had initiated the stop had to ask for additional reinforcements as they tried to extricate themselves from what was an increasingly volatile situation. Plastic bullets were fired as they attempted to control the large and aggressive crowd.

Armalite Rifle

Whilst perusing my old Notebook's from that particular time, I came across a very brief note which perhaps will help illustrate just how bizarre life was for police officers in Springfield Road back then. The note simply records that at 6:30 p.m. on the evening of Friday, May 15, 1981, at our pre duty briefing we had a 'lecture by army re. RPG7. Major ****.' This was of course the very next night after the murder of our colleague Sam Vallely.

After forty odd years, unsurprisingly I can't really remember any of the finer details of that lecture. However, I do remember very well the gist of what he was saying. In particular he was addressing those of us who were the drivers of the station Land Rovers, when he advised that we shouldn't at any time allow our vehicles to get isolated out on open ground. He also stressed the need to be mobile at all times, during our periods of patrol. The reasoning behind those words of advice wasn't difficult to work out, however putting them into practice, especially the bit about always being on the move, would obviously have been more challenging.

When you take a moment to consider what was actually happening in that lecture, it really was a most bizarre and surreal experience!

Here we were, civilian police officers in the UK being lectured by a British Army weapons expert, on how best we could avoid being victims of a Russian made anti-tank weapon, on the inner-city streets of our country's capital city!

As ever, police managed to find humour in what really wasn't a very humorous situation! I recall everyone joking about just how in our armour-plated Hotspur vehicles, we ought to approach the main Falls, Grosvenor, Springfield Road crossroads at the next 9 a.m. rush hour, without stopping!

CHAPTER 16

Plastics or Live Rounds?

Diary Date:	May 1981.
Incident:	Electrical Fault in Bravo Delta Eight Zero.
Background:	12 Hour Shifts for Hunger Strike.
Storyteller:	Don.

Whilst on a 7 p.m. to 7 a.m. night shift duty, which occurred sometime in late May of 1981, I was the driver of the mobile police patrol vehicle Bravo Delta Eight Zero, working out of Springfield Road RUC Station. That particular night, which was during the IRA Hunger Strike campaign, we were actually part of a three-vehicle patrol, as along with another police mobile (Bravo Delta Eight One) we were also accompanied by a military Land Rover.

It was during our pre-duty briefing in the station, we were informed that our vehicle crew would be accompanied by and be under the supervision of our station Chief Inspector. As our briefing continued, it was made clear to us that part of our responsibility that evening was to ensure that the main arterial routes of the division remained open at all times. Our patrol's specific area of responsibility would include Springfield Road, with particular attention to be given to the area from around the West Circular Road, up to its junction with Whiterock Road.

That portion of the Springfield Road, from the West Circular up, measures about three-quarters of a mile, maybe a little more. On the face of it, it may seem that it really shouldn't be a major issue for three well manned security force patrol vehicles, to keep traffic flowing along that relatively small area. However!

To put what may at first glance, seem to be a fairly routine and undemanding task into proper context, for the benefit of the reader I will elaborate a little on the 'lay of the land,' as it was at that time was the height of the Troubles.

Rioters on the Springfield Road, not far from New Barnsley Station, May 1981

Back then and indeed to this day, that part of the Springfield Road to a greater or lesser extent is bordered on both sides by major housing developments. Immediately on your right, as you travel country-wards on the Springfield from the West Circular, is the Highfield Estate. Almost exclusively Protestant and Unionist, at that time there would have been little or no threat toward security force personnel or their vehicles from that location. The Highfield was bordered on its upper end by the Springmartin Road, and loosely speaking was the last point where security force members would consider themselves safe, before venturing into what would be openly hostile republican areas.

After passing the Springmartin Road, almost immediately on the left is Springhill Avenue. It leads from the main Springfield, down into the very heart of what is a staunchly catholic and republican estate, Ballymurphy. That sprawling development extends from the Springfield right across to the Whiterock Road, and as a consequence bordered our area of responsibility.

Continuing country-wards, on the right-hand side of Springfield Road, are another two major housing estates, Moyard and New Barnsley. Like the 'Murph,' these two developments were republican strongholds and consequently unwelcoming and hostile to the security forces.

Amazingly squeezed in between these developments, on the right-hand side of and facing onto the main Springfield Road, was the small but heavily fortified and well-guarded army and police base of New Barnsley station. To security force patrols, this station was almost like a little oasis of relative safety, in what at that time was a very barren and dangerous landscape! It was totally surrounded by a populace which at best would have been non-plussed towards its very existence!

But let's be frank, in all honesty I think a more accurate description of New Barnsley station back then, would be to liken it to the 'Alamo!' It was surrounded: front, back, left and right by residents who would have been ill-disposed and hostile towards them! It was seemingly under a constant barrage of bricks, bottles and petrol bombs. This 'outpost,' within our country's capital city, was also a regular target for gun, rocket, mortar and blast bomb attacks!

I'm guessing many folks reading this, particularly the younger generation, will perhaps be feeling that my description of this area is overly dramatic or simply over the top! I can assure you that my portrayal of this area at that time is authentic.

Anyway, to get back to the story of the incident which occurred to our Bravo Delta Eight Zero callsign that particular evening. The lower part of our patrol area, between the West Circular and up to New Barnsley station was that evening unusually quiet. Consequently, it required only passing attention from our patrol vehicles. Unfortunately, that wasn't the case with the upper end! The area surrounding New Barnsley station, up to its junction with the Whiterock Road, (Kelly's Corner) was in a state of absolute mayhem! Huge crowds, hundreds if not thousands of rioters were stoning and petrol bombing anything that moved.

The rioters, who to a man wore masks or balaclavas, were trying to hijack any vehicle which had the misfortune of travelling along that particular stretch of the road. No doubt had they succeeded in commandeering such a vehicle; it would subsequently have been set alight and used as a barricade to block the main thoroughfare. By maintaining our mobile patrols up and down the road, we at least ensured that we kept the main road open.

However, in doing so we undoubtedly made ourselves attractive targets for those who were interested in participating in such activities, which let me tell you were innumerable! The gangs of rioters seemed to ebb and flow out of the nearby housing estates. Each time we passed, our vehicles were ambushed by a swarm of rioters, who battered us in ever-increasing waves of bricks, bottles and what seemed to be an endless supply of petrol bombs!

Our patrol route was very predictable! The convoy of three vehicles would travel down as far as New Barnsley station, before executing a turn in the station gateway. Then we would drive back up the road to a small turning circle, which was just on the countryside of Kelly's corner. This short and circuitous route ensured we had a continuous presence on this part of the road.

On what we all thought was just going to be another routine run from the top end, back down towards New Barnsley, I remember our vehicles had got out of sequence. From being the lead vehicle with our Chief Inspector on board, somehow or other we had actually become 'tail end

Charlie,' last in the line. I don't remember how this happened, there certainly wasn't any conscious or deliberate reason for it!

As we drove citywards and just after passing through the junction at Kelly's corner, I remember noticing what seemed to be a particularly large crowd of petrol bombers, attacking us on our near side, the left-hand side of our vehicle. Our vehicle crew that night, besides myself and our Chief, also included an additional two colleagues. Their role as extra-observers in the rear of our patrol vehicle, included each being armed with FRGs. Undoubtedly better known as a plastic-bullet gun, the Federal Riot Gun was used extensively and to great effect over the Hunger Strike campaign. However, experience and training told us that for them to be used effectively, they really had to be aimed and fired from a static vehicle. So, to that end and in the face of what was an onslaught of rioters who were absolutely pummelling us, I remember very deliberately slowing our vehicle way down, before pausing completely.

I should add that this incident actually took place around a fortnight after a very dear friend and greatly valued colleague Constable Samuel Vallely,[6] had been killed at the same location. My thoughts were, if they could hit his Land Rover with an RPG7 rocket, they could hit us where we were sitting. Consequently, my intention was that this stop would be very, very brief!

Having readied themselves for this, the two rear gunners reacted immediately! Jumping from their inward facing, seated on their bum position, they quickly turned their bodies to face the near side of our Hotspur. By spinning round, they were then able to kneel in a much more upright position on the rear side bench seats. This posture allowed them to open the small firing hatches, see out the side of the vehicle, and by doing so easily identify their targets. Having done this and with our vehicle now static and steady, they took aim before rattling off a couple of shots, which had the desired effect of driving the crowd back!

---

6   See Chapter 15, The Ultimate Sacrifice.

Just as soon as I heard the two shots, followed by the noise of the small firing hatches being slammed shut, I made to put the vehicle back into gear and get us on our way again. However, I soon realised that something was very wrong. Everything in our vehicle had gone totally blank! Absolutely everything! It seemed that both the mechanical and the electrical systems of the vehicle, had just cut out! We were stuck! Our vehicle was immobile, and as our radio system was electrical, it was also 'kaput!' This of course meant that we had no way of calling for assistance. After exchanging nervous glances with our Chief, I remember looking out at the growing crowd of rioters which after initially retreating, were by now getting ever closer to our vehicle.

Recognising our plight, the two gunners again threw open the rear-firing hatches, allowing them to fire some more plastic bullets at the lead protagonists of the crowd. As was always the case, the sight of the hatches being opened and the sound of the plastic bullets being fired, had the crowd running for cover. But almost as quickly, they were back into attack mode and again moving menacingly towards our stranded truck!

As the seconds ticked away it seemed that our vehicle was about to be totally engulfed by the crowds! The guys with the baton guns were doing their best, but it seemed that they had slowed down their rate of fire. The consequence of which was that the rioters were getting to almost within touching distance! I'll never forget hearing one of those guys in the back of our vehicle screaming at our Chief Inspector, "Chief, we are down to our last two plastic bullets!" before continuing, "Can we use live ammunition?"

The Chief, who at that point was busying himself trying to contact our control room, via his pocket radio, understandably was taking just a minute or two to consider that question and the serious implications of his reply! I then reached across and grabbed hold of the pocket radio from him, as he just didn't seem able to get it to transmit. For no logical reason, other than the crowd attacking us on our near side, I chose to push the driver's door open a little bit, before leaning out with the radio and trying to see if it would work that way.

Thankfully, after turning it off and on (technically known as 'rebooting' nowadays) it burst into life. Unfortunately, our own 'B' Division radio channel was chalk-a-block with chatter, which meant I had no way of getting airspace! I quickly changed the radio channel and found myself on the 'A' Division radio net, where I immediately identified myself and asked their controller for help. Initially, he seemed quite perturbed that a 'B' division call sign had dared to have chosen their 'A' division net, and he almost rebuffed me for doing so. However, after a few highly inappropriate words were exchanged, he quickly got the message and radioed our other call signs for assistance!

Our second police vehicle, accompanied by its military escort, were very quickly back on the scene. After both of these crews had fired a fresh 'salvo' of plastic bullets, they were able to draw up alongside us. A brief dialogue between myself and the other police driver concluded that, given the situation we were in, the best we could do was for their vehicle to push us down the hill towards the safety of New Barnsley station, about 200 metres away. But just as soon as their vehicle had given ours a bit of a shove and we began rolling down the slight hill, miraculously the electrics came back on. We were then able to 'fire up' our vehicle and get going again under our own steam.

As I mentioned before, in the big picture of police incidents during the IRA Hunger Strike, this won't go down in history as a momentous event. To be perfectly honest, it didn't even warrant a written entry in my police notebook! However, I can honestly say that at times during those tense and frightening five or six minutes, I really did wonder was I going to see home again.

CHAPTER 17

Contact, Contact at the 'Colins!'

Diary Date:	May 22, 1981.
Incident:	Shots Fired at Police Springfield Road/Colins Area.
Background:	12 Hour Shifts for Hunger Strike.
Storyteller:	Andrew.

At 6.30 p.m. on the evening of Friday May 22, 1981, I reported for duty at Springfield Road RUC Station. As preparation for our upcoming night shift, we would routinely be briefed regarding any events of significance that had occurred during the previous shift and then we would be detailed as to what our precise duty would be. My specific role that evening was to be the driver of Bravo Delta Eight Zero, which accompanied by Bravo Delta Eight One, would operate as a two-vehicle mobile patrol.

The first part of that evening's shift was relatively uneventful, with nothing of any real consequence occurring. That was until the early hours of the following morning. At 1:45am I was driving the vehicle citywards on Springfield Road, approaching an area on our right, which we referred to as the 'Colin's.'[7]

---

7   The streets of Colinward, Colinpark and Colinview.

Back then, at this point on the main Springfield Road, the footpaths were especially wide. As we were approaching the area of Colinview Street, I noticed that there was a large builder's skip sitting on the path and that there were several male persons standing about the footpath, convenient to the skip. As we approached, I saw those individuals reach into the skip and lift out bricks and bottles which they proceeded to hurl at our vehicle.

Immediately I accelerated and drove my vehicle up onto the pavement in an effort to detain those who were responsible. However, just as quickly as the attack started, it stopped. The culprits quickly made off, disappearing into the side streets and alleyways. By this point, the crews of our two vehicles had dismounted and were giving chase on foot. Whilst I remained with the vehicle, my colleagues gave chase and almost immediately became unsighted to me. However, within what seemed like seconds, the frightening sound of gunfire rang out! I immediately reported this 'Contact' to our control room, and then started the agonising wait for my colleagues to return to our vehicles!

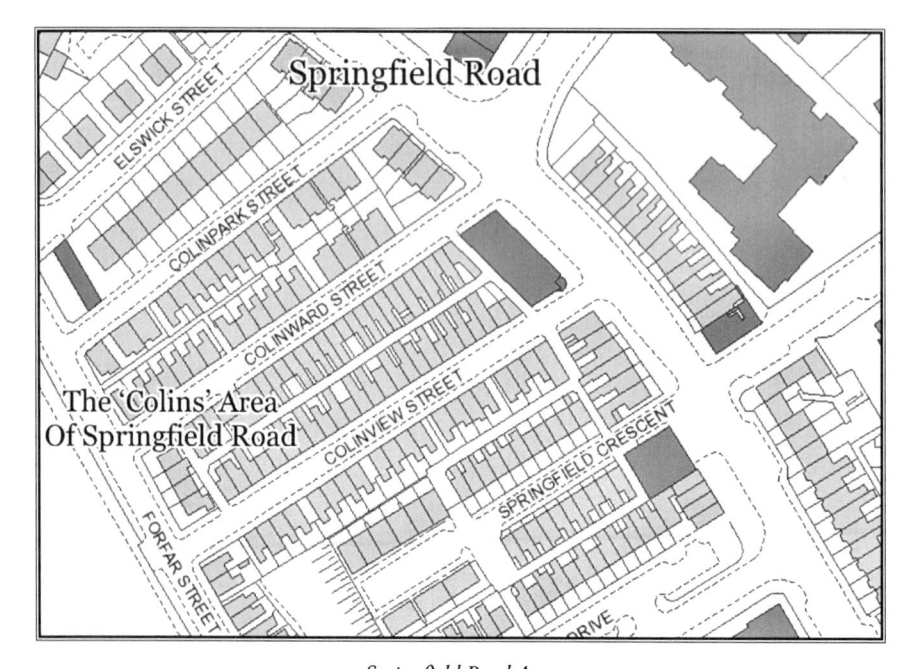

Springfield Road Area

Thankfully, within just a few minutes they had all returned, with no one any the worse for the experience. We then made our way back to Springfield Road Station. Several of my colleagues reported having been involved in a brief exchange of gunfire with an armed man. They related how whilst pursuing the 'missile throwers' through the dark side-streets, they encountered a gunman who had shot at them.

Postscript

Unbeknownst to us, sometime after that exchange of gunfire, an ambulance was called to attend to a 21-year-old man suffering from gunshot wounds, in Elswick Street. The injured man was taken to the casualty department of the Royal Victoria Hospital, where he was admitted. Elswick Street was the next street to Colinpark Street.

CHAPTER 18

Member Caught in Terrorist Blast Bomb Attack.

Diary Date:	8th July 1981.
Incident:	Blast Bomb Attack Springhill Avenue.
Background:	12 Hour Shifts for Hunger Strike.
Storyteller:	Andrew.

This specific story ultimately relates to an incident which occurred on the evening of Wednesday July 8, 1981. However, to help with context and enable me to paint a fuller picture of what life was like for Springfield Road police officers caught up in the IRA Hunger Strike campaign, I have included some background detail from the previous nights turn of duty.

The previous evening, Tuesday July 7, along with the other members of my section, I had reported to Springfield Road for a 12-hour night shift duty. We spent all of that evening and the early hours of Wednesday morning carrying out general patrols of our area. At 5:11 a.m. on Wednesday morning, Joe McDonnell became the fifth of the IRA Hunger Strikers to die.

Just prior to that time and having spent most of the previous evening and mornings duty patrolling our area, our crews took time out to call into the station for a brief break and a warm cup of tea. It was just as we were sitting around in our recreation room having that 'cuppa,' that we were to learn of McDonnell's death, in what was a very traditional West Belfast fashion.

Breaking through the quiet of the early morning stillness, came the unmistakable grating noise of banging bin-lids and high-pitched whistles. As the news of his death broke, and initially in small groups of one's and two's, the local residents left their houses and came out onto the neighbourhood streets. In what was a very basic and simple manner, they then noisily and repeatedly banged the bin-lids of their metal household waste bins, on the road. The noise of this clatter was also accompanied by the participants blowing whistles! A rudimentary neighbourhood alert system, which has been used in republican areas throughout the years.

As I mentioned earlier, this was a very basic practice, but it must also be acknowledged that it was a really effective way to alert the local community that their presence was needed on the street! Almost like jungle drums, this community alert system started with a whisper, but within a very short period of time it was like thunder, as the whole area seemed to have joined in! The fluid like ripple effect of this 'call to arms,' went from street to street and from one neighbourhood to another. Within a very short space of time, there was literally thousands on the streets. And it's safe to say that not all who came onto the streets in response to the noise of the bin-lids, were participating in practices as innocent as banging bin lids!

Sounding the Alarm

Heavy rioting broke out almost immediately and continued throughout the day, with the police and army struggling to contain the violence wherever it broke out. This was evidenced by the fact that our shift, which was scheduled to finish at 7 a.m., didn't actually get finished until 10:30 a.m., due to the severity of the rioting.

When we were eventually relieved from our duties, we all headed to our separate homes to catch up on some much-needed sleep, before returning to duty again at 6:30 p.m that Wednesday evening, for another night 'in the trenches!' That night I was detailed as observer in Bravo Delta Eight Zero, and informed that our own section inspector would be accompanying us throughout our turn of duty.

A particular area of trouble in the early part of that Wednesday evening seemed to be around the top part of Springfield Road, near its junctions with Springmartin Road and Springhill Avenue. Whilst not directly opposite each other geographically, the two roads I've mentioned above, were undoubtedly directly opposite each other in the political spectrum of Northern Ireland. Springmartin Road was predominantly

Unionist and Protestant, whilst Springhill Avenue, an access road into the Ballymurphy Estate, besides being a primarily Roman Catholic area was also a Republican stronghold.

Back then, located just below the Springhill Avenue junction with the Springfield Road, was a large builder supply yard, JP Corry's. It seemed to store an enormous amount of wood for the building trade, and as such became a real target for the rioters from the Ballymurphy area, who seemed hell-bent on setting it ablaze!

Hence the early part of that night's duty was spent in that general area, either trying to keep the opposing factions apart, or trying to stop the republican rioters from gaining access to the timber yard. The practicalities of both these tasks saw us 'lie-up' in our Land Rover's about 100 yards or so further down the main road, where we were relatively safe! We literally sat in our vehicles watching the main road, only moving forward when either of the two crowds emerged from their own areas out onto the main Springfield Road. When either emerged, we would just move forward, and it seemed our presence was enough to cause the crowds to sink back into their own areas.

It just became a game of cat and mouse which we didn't dare to take our eyes off, as the potential consequences of missing out could easily cost someone their life. The only real difference when we moved forward to push either side back into their particular area, was that when we moved towards the rioters from the Springhill area, we would inevitably come under an attack of bricks and petrol bombs. This remained the situation that evening until around 10:30 p.m. when I remember that darkness had fallen. Obviously as it was July, it wasn't a real pitch dark like you would get on a winter's night, but it was dark enough that we were no longer able to see people unless they were close to artificial lights. As we would find out very soon, it was also dark enough for an IRA terrorist to mingle unseen within the crowds, from where he could launch his attempt at murdering members of the Police.

As we kept watch from our vantage point a little further down the Springfield Road, we noticed a crowd of youths emerging from Springhill Avenue and they seemed to be making their way across the main road towards Springmartin. They were carrying petrol bombs in their hands, clearly with the intention of launching an attack into that area. Our vehicles immediately sped forward, stopping to allow us to get out of the vehicles in an effort to pursue those holding the petrol bombs. As ever, they had seen us coming and quickly ran back into their safe area of Springhill Avenue. Once there, they continued with their stone and petrol bomb attacks on our vehicles.

Unbeknownst to us, the last crowds foray out onto the Springfield Road, had been nothing but a 'come-on,' an attempt to draw us out into the open. The crowd was by this stage gathered some distance down Springhill Avenue, from where they were throwing stones and petrol bombs at us. At that time there was a large metal gate across the top of Springhill Avenue. Essentially placed there to prevent 'murder gangs,' having easy vehicular access, it unfortunately also prevented us from pursuing the rioters into the area. Now under the cover of darkness and safe in the knowledge that our vehicle couldn't pursue them beyond the security gate, they continued to blitz us with any object they could get their hands on.

However, what we didn't know was that members of the Ballymurphy IRA were about to use the cover of darkness and the ongoing riot, for a much more sinister attack. From out of the darkness, someone in the crowd threw what we now know to have been a homemade 'blast-bomb!' As we were standing at our vehicle it exploded, basically with a similar force to that of a hand grenade. Thankfully, it had actually rolled directly below our Land Rover which absorbed some of the device's explosive force.

I had been standing fairly close to the back of our vehicle and got blown off my feet, landing on my backside a few yards back. Adrenaline undoubtedly saw me jump back up and onto my feet, telling my colleagues that I was fine and there was nothing to worry about.

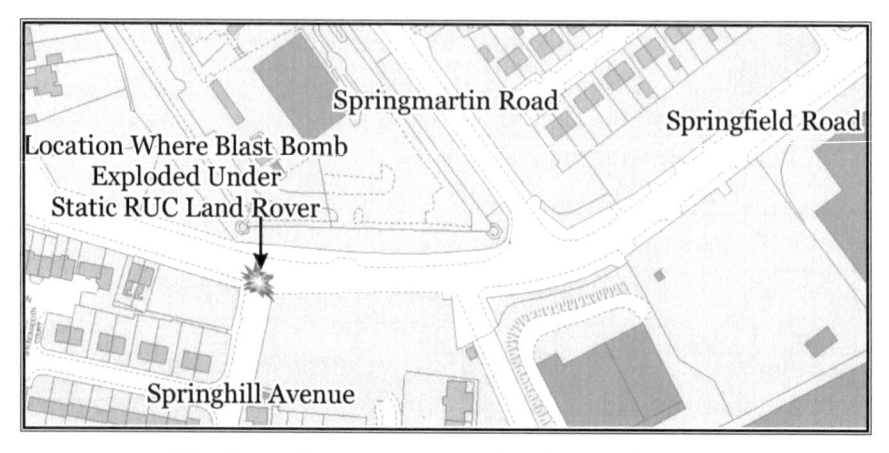

Map showing the approximate area of attack, Springfield Road.

To this day I don't know why or indeed how we got there, but our vehicle then made its way to the casualty department in the Royal Victoria Hospital, which was only a 5–10-minute drive away. By the time we got there, it was clear to everyone that I was suffering some sort of aftershock from the explosion. I was feeling really groggy, and I remember being shepherded into a treatment room where I was attended by a doctor. A quick diagnosis of concussion, eventually saw me sent home from work under the care of the New Barnsley Station Sergeant, who drove me home in his private car, which oddly enough I remember as being a cream-coloured Fiat Mirafiori with a vinyl roof!

After a few hours' sleep, I was soon up and about with no aftereffects, allowing me to return to work that night. The camaraderie within the Police back then was on a different level. By taking time off work it might have meant that you would miss something that your friends and colleagues were involved in. I really didn't want that to happen!

Postscript

It was reported at the time that the sickness levels within the RUC during the 1980-81 IRA Hunger Strike campaign, was an all-time low.

CHAPTER 19

First Hunger Striker to Break the Fast.

Diary Date:	July 31, 1981.
Incident:	First Hunger Striker To Give Up.
Background:	12 Hour Shifts for Hunger Strike.
Storyteller:	Andrew.

On the morning of Friday July 31, 1981, I reported for duty in Springfield Road RUC Station. At that morning's pre-duty briefing I was detailed to drive the station mobile patrol vehicle Bravo Delta Eight Zero. I can't recall the exact time, but at one point during the day, we received a radio message from our station controller at Bravo Delta instructing us to return to base immediately to pick up our section Inspector, Bravo Delta 6.

We weren't informed what the tasking was at that point, but simply to return to Springfield Road as quickly as possible. Just as we drove in through the heavy station security gates, we noticed that our Inspector was already out in the station yard waiting for us! He quickly climbed aboard our vehicle and took up his position in the observers' seat, before directing me to drive up towards the M1 motorway junction with Kennedy Way/Stockmans Lane.

Once we were back underway again, he went on to explain just what our tasking was and why it hadn't been broadcast over the radio-net! He explained that although the news hadn't at that point been made public, one of the Republican Hunger Strikers (the first to do so) had been taken off the fast and that he was just then in an ambulance en route to Musgrave Park Hospital.[8] That ambulance which was heading citywards on the motorway having left the Maze prison, was currently being escorted by Police in a soft skin vehicle. Our tasking was simple, as we were in an armour-plated Hotspur, we were to replace the more vulnerable soft skin vehicle at that pre-arranged rendezvous point.

We parked up and waited at a point convenient to the slip road, which runs off the motorway and down into the Stockmans Lane/Kennedy Way roundabout. We didn't have to wait too long before the ambulance arrived, closely followed by its Police escort.

On the roundabout they dutifully held back, allowing me to drive our vehicle into a position which was immediately behind the ambulance, before they broke off and headed away back country-wards on the motorway. Our role was short and sweet! We literally had nothing else to do but escort the ambulance from that roundabout, for around a quarter of a mile up Stockmans Lane, and into the security of the military wing of Musgrave Park Hospital.

On arrival there, I drove our Land Rover, nose first, fairly close to the hospital wall to shield and protect the back doors of the ambulance, when it reversed up to the loading bay area. Our Inspector jumped out and went over to chat to those who were waiting to help with unloading the stretcher. I remember thinking that it seemed to be a fairly strong welcoming party for the patient.

I couldn't help thinking that this could actually be a historic moment, possibly the beginning of the end of the Hunger Strike. With that in

---

8 The hospital opened in 1920. The United States Army constructed nissen huts on the site during the Second World War to create a temporary base for soldiers preparing to take part in the Normandy Landings. During the Troubles it was a military hospital for soldiers and terrorists that were injured.

mind, I grabbed my camera and snapped the attached photo which has never been seen before.

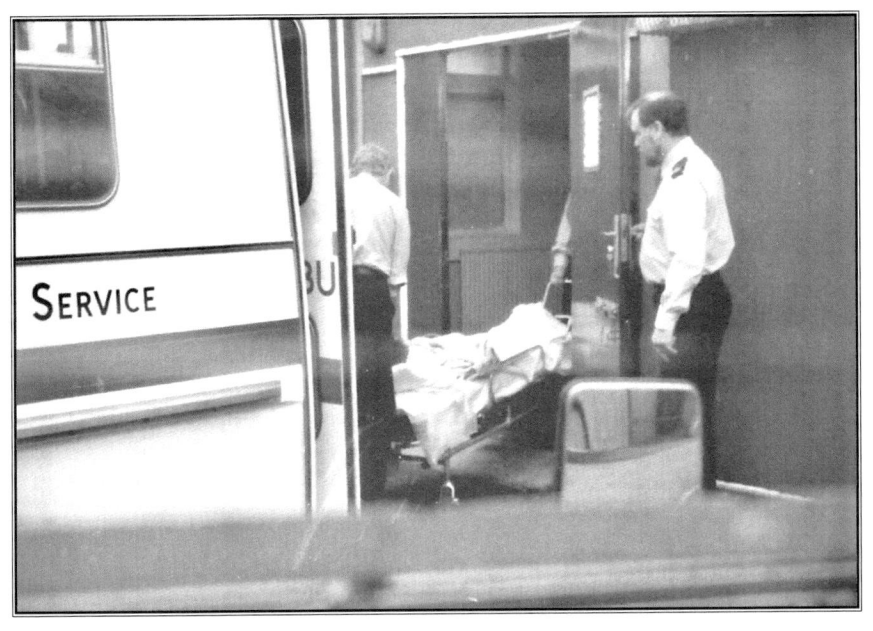

One of the first hunger strikers who came off the hunger strike

CHAPTER 20

Never, Ever, Forget Their Sacrifice

Diary Date:	June 15, 1984.
Incident:	Murder of Constable Michael Todd.
Background:	Planned Search in Lenadoon.
Storyteller:	Samuel.

Constable Michael Todd, age 22.
Murdered by terrorists June 15, 1984

Queen's Gallantry Medal
Awarded for exemplary acts of bravery

At around 10:45 p.m. on Thursday June 15, 1984, I reported for duty at Springfield Road RUC Station. My role that night was to act as a member of the station mobile patrol vehicle, Bravo Delta Eight Zero. The early part of the shift was comparatively quiet, so as was often the case on Night shift, we took the opportunity to head across the city to

Castlereagh Station, which operated the country's only 24-hour police canteen. Besides allowing us to enjoy some hot food, it also enabled us to have a bit of a change of scenery.

At some point before our crew headed across to Castlereagh, It may even have been at our pre-duty briefing, I remember being informed that our colleagues from Woodbourne and Andersonstown stations, would later that morning be involved in a planned search operation in the Lenadoon area. As this had little or no bearing on us, we continued with our plan and drove over to Castlereagh.

It was only when we had finished our meal-break and as we were leisurely making our way back over towards our own 'patch,' that we became aware that something had gone terribly wrong out in Lenadoon. Our vehicle's police radio which had thankfully been very quiet for most of the night, suddenly burst into life. To be honest, the precise content of the radio transmission was almost unintelligible.

A very stressed and clearly panicked member was trying to transmit from the scene of the search in Lenadoon Avenue. Whilst the precise detail of that intended message was obscure, it was however crystal clear that something had gone dreadfully wrong at that planned search. We made our way to that location just as quickly as we could!

As we arrived, an ambulance was passing us going in the other direction, which of course is never a good sign. On entering the front door of the premises where the incident had taken place, I noticed the floor was sodden with pools of blood. The hallway was littered with discarded bloody field dressings, which I assumed had been used by the ambulance paramedics. In a room immediately to my left, I saw an armed colleague 'covering' a man who appeared to be hysterical! He was screaming at the top of his voice at the Sergeant, "Don't shoot me, don't shoot me!"

I then arrived at the main living room of the house, which seemed to be crowded with both civilians and uniformed police. I walked on through to one of the bedrooms where I saw the body of a man lying in a large pool of blood, beside him was what appeared to be an AK-47 assault rifle, officially known as the Avtomat Kalashnikova.

He was half naked, dressed only in a pair of jeans with no top on, although I did note that he had what looked like a pair of socks covering his hands. He had a huge hole in the side of his head.

We remained at the scene for some time until all the necessary police agencies arrived to proceed with the follow-up investigation. Then, we were involved transporting some of those who had been arrested, over to Castlereagh Holding Centre.

I should add that just as I was about to leave the flat, I actually noticed a police officer sitting in the bedroom where I had earlier seen the half-naked body. When I went in to check just what he was up to, I saw that he was actually kneeling down beside the body and holding the man's wrist. I asked him what he was doing, and seemingly quite logically he replied, "I'm feeling for a pulse." Conscious that this was a young guy who had just seen three of his colleagues literally 'riddled' by an AK-47 assault rifle, I recognised that he was in a state of shock. I gently pulled his hand away, pointing out that the man was dead and there was nothing we could do for him.

Postscript

First published in 1999, 'Lost Lives, the stories of the men, women and children who died as a result of the Northern Ireland troubles,' is unquestionably the definitive reference book regarding this subject matter. The coauthors spent seven years researching the stories behind every 'Troubles' related death, before in this unique book publishing a brief summary of each. It's to this source, along with the contemporary news media, that I turn to to help flesh-out the story of that morning's incident.

At around 3 a.m. on the morning of Friday June 15, 1984, members of the Army and the RUC undertook what was expected to be a fairly routine, intelligence led, search and arrest operation on a flat in Lenadoon Avenue. Police initially made their way to the front door of the property, and despite several 'noisy' attempts to raise or awaken those within the flat, were ultimately unable to get any response.

Faced with what was obviously a totally unsatisfactory outcome, two of the officers, Constable Michael Todd and his supervising Sergeant, then tried to physically force entry through the front door. It appears that whilst they were able to force the door's lock, due to the fact that those inside had wedged a central heating radiator in behind the door, they just weren't able to force it open wide enough to allow them unfettered access.

As they continued trying to push their way through what seemed to be a stubbornly jammed door, they heard someone from within the flat shouting, "It's the peelers, use the AK-47 and shoot them!" The retelling of the facts of this story which is recorded in the 'Lost Lives' book, report that it had actually been well-known republican Gino Gallagher, who had shouted that murderous instruction to the gunman Paul 'Bonanza' McCann, just before the shooting began

Before the police officers were able to react to the imminent danger, two thunderous bursts of gunfire erupted from inside the flat! Michael Todd and two other constables were each struck multiple times sustaining serious injuries. Despite the seriousness of those injuries, amazingly the other two officers survived. Sadly Michael, who had been hit three times by the high-velocity bullets of the AK-47, died as a result of his injuries.

When the gunfire had stopped, and the police had eventually gained full access to the flat, they made a startling discovery. Inside they found what an RUC Chief Inspector would later describe as being, "an outlawed INLA hideout." The gunman, Paul 'Bonanza' McCann, was found lying in a pool of his own blood. Wearing only a pair of jeans, he had a serious gunshot wound to his head. His hands which were covered with a pair of socks, were still holding the AK-47 rifle, which lay beside him.

AK-47

Six days after the incident, three men and a pregnant woman were each charged with the murder of Michael Todd. It was reported in the news media that during the court proceedings, the four accused actually 'laughed and joked among themselves.'

The inquest pertaining to the deaths of Michael Todd and Paul McCann was held at Belfast Coroners Court, some three years later in May, 1987. The Coroner Mr James Elliot, on hearing the evidence presented to him paid tribute to the police 'heroism' during the operation, which cost one of their colleagues his life. The evidence he heard was consistent to that which had been reported in the press at the time of the incident. It had been Paul McCann who had fired two bursts of gunfire at the police that morning, and each of those salvos were of eleven rounds.

Michael Todd was hit by three rounds, two of which were fatal. The other two constables who were shot but miraculously survived, had also sustained life-threatening injuries. These officers' injuries included having been shot in both legs and a cheek, and secondly in both the stomach and a leg.

Both Michael Todd, posthumously, and Sergeant Thomas Saunders were awarded the Queens Gallantry Medal for their actions on the day of the Lenadoon incident.

A forensic scientist was able to confirm to the coroner that it had been McCann who had fired the AK-47 and that he had been killed by a bullet fired from his gun. He further explained that the rifle had the words 'Black Widow,' burned into its wooden butt.

No firearms were discharged by the security forces during that morning's operation.

CHAPTER 21

The Murder of an Artist

Diary Date:	October 12, 1986.
Incident:	Murder of RUC Officer Desi Dobbin.
Background:	Mortar Attack on New Barnsley RUC Station.
Storyteller:	Andrew.

Desmond (Desi) Dobbin, age 42. Murdered by terrorists. October 12, 1986.

Desmond Dobbin, or Desi to his friends, had two loves in his life. The first was his family, which included his wife of 14 years and their two children, a 10-year-old son and a 5-year-old daughter. His second love was art, which is why he became an art teacher before joining the RUC. His work was displayed in numerous RUC stations throughout Northern Ireland.

On the evening of Saturday October 11, 1986, Desi was performing security duties at New Barnsley RUC Station, on the Springfield Road. At 10:03 p.m. he left what was the well protected and relatively safe cover of one of the stations heavily fortified security sangars, with the intention of walking across the open station yard towards another of the stations sangars. At what was the most inopportune moment, a group of IRA terrorists launched a home-made mortar bomb towards the Station. Caught out in the open yard when the mortar exploded in midair above their heads, Desi and another colleague, both sustained serious injuries. Whilst his colleague made a good recovery, regrettably Desi's injuries proved to be much more serious, and he passed away just three hours later.

Desi, with full police honours, was buried from Townsend Street Presbyterian Church Belfast on October 14.

A year and a half after Desi's murder, the inquest looking into the circumstances of how he lost his life, was held in Belfast Coroners Court. Coroner James Elliot went on to describe, "how 60 seconds was the difference between life and death." Elaborating Mr Elliot explained how if Desi had only left the safety of the security sangar, "either one minute earlier or one minute later," it was highly probable that he would still be alive! The inquest further heard how the terrorists, from a small alleyway off Glenalina Road in the Ballymurphy estate, had launched their murderous attack. Using almost '3 stones (20kg) of volatile home-made explosives,' packed into a 'sawn off pub gas cylinder,' the improvised mortar had been detonated using a 'transistor radio battery.'

Postscript

In what amounts to an extremely sad postscript to this particular story, is the fact that some 4 years after surviving the mortar attack on New Barnsley, Desi's colleague was also murdered in yet another terrorist atrocity.

On the morning of June 6, 1990, ex RUC Reserve Constable James Sefton, who had retired from the police service after recovering from the injuries he sustained in the 1986 New Barnsley mortar attack, accompanied by his wife Ellen got into the family car outside their home. They hadn't travelled far when a UCBT (under car booby trap) bomb, planted by members of the IRA, exploded. The explosion ripped through the car causing catastrophic injuries to both of the unsuspecting innocent victims. The damage was such that Ellen and James had to be cut-out of the wreckage of the severely damaged car. Sadly, James died later that same day whilst being treated in hospital. His wife Ellen also succumbed to her injuries just a day later, and both were buried in a double funeral on June 12, from St Matthews Parish Church, Belfast.

Two of the illustrations which I consider myself very fortunate to have been given permission to use, are actually copies of original artwork which hold a special place in the heart of many RUC men and women from that most difficult era.

Falls Road, Belfast. Painting by Desmond (Desi) Dobbin. Murdered October 11, 1986.

Desi's two pictures, illustrate both the inside of what was a very 'homely looking' Hastings Street RUC Station Guard Room, (used in an earlier chapter) and then a much more graphic image of an RUC Land Rover crew in action on the Falls Road close to its junction with Leeson Street. See Above.

CHAPTER 22

Heavy Gun Battle at New Barnsley.

Diary Date:	July 13, 1996.
Incident:	Attempted Murder of Police at New Barnsley.
Background:	Drumcree Standoff.
Storyteller:	Gareth.

Background to Incident

Following what was a hotly disputed Orange Order parade which took place, to and from Drumcree Parish Church Portadown in July 1995, one year later tensions surrounding this annual parade were again running high. As the date of the parade approached, July 7th, and with no agreement in place, the determination regarding it was left to the RUC Chief Constable, Hugh Annesley. Initially his decision, given on July 6, was that he would not permit the Portadown Orange Order to return home via the predominantly Roman Catholic Garvaghy Road.

However, circumstances were to conspire which would ultimately see the Chief Constable forced to go back on that initial decision. Consequently, around noon on the evening of July 11, he announced that he had reversed his earlier decision. The fallout of that change, saw large numbers of heavily armoured police and military personnel escort around 1,200 Orangemen from Drumcree Parish Church back to Portadown, via the Garvaghy Road. It seemed that the whole country, which even in the lead up to this occurrence had been like a powder-keg, literally exploded!

The rights and wrongs, and the reasons for and against this last-minute change are of course open to debate, however, here isn't the place for that discourse. Enough to know, that the incident which I'm about to retell in this story, came about as a consequence of that decision and the street disorder which followed it.

Before beginning my retelling of this incident, I'm very conscious that there may be some people reading this who perhaps aren't totally familiar with the unique nuances of Northern Ireland, it's politics and it's policing. So perhaps, admittedly slightly tongue in cheek, it would be helpful if I took just a moment to clarify the repercussions and the consequences of decisions such as those which were taken during that long hot summer of 1996!

Unsurprisingly, considering we are talking about Northern Ireland and there's rarely a sensible compromise to any problem, it all boils down to,

An 'Either' – 'Or,' situation.

Either allow the parade to proceed down the Garvaghy Road, which would please the Loyalists, but really antagonise the Republicans. (Outcome, Republicans would batter the police!)

Or

Ban the parade from proceeding down the Garvaghy Road, which would please the Republicans, but really antagonise the Loyalists. (Outcome, Loyalists would batter the police!)

The inevitable consequence of 'Either, Or,' was always going to be – The police getting battered!

Incident

On the morning of July 13, 1996, I was a Sergeant in charge of a Land Rover patrol vehicle working in 'B' Division, West Belfast. Shortly after midnight, we received a tasking via a radio transmission from Belfast Regional Control, to make our way to New Barnsley Station as quickly as we could. We weren't exactly sure just what we would be driving into, as the initial report seemed to suggest that there was a genuine fear that the station was in danger of being overrun by rioters. But, given that our vehicle was one of eleven (yes 11) Land Rover crews which had also just been tasked to this incident, (7 RUC and 4 Military) we were in no doubt that it was a grave situation!

On arrival, to help us better assess just what it was we were driving into, we pulled to a stop about 70 or 80 metres short of the station, where we manoeuvred our vehicles side-by-side across the full breadth of the main road. The scene which we then witnessed, even from that distance, was quite honestly like nothing I'd ever seen before! Or thankfully since!

It almost resembled something out of the Mad Max movie films! There were enormous crowds of marauding rioters blocking the main thoroughfare of the Springfield Road, it was totally impassable. It seemed the rioters were literally swarming all over the beleaguered station. Whilst armed with petrol bombs, they were easily scaling the perimeter wall.

I noticed that even the Super Sangar, the high Station Sanger, which was surrounded by heavy-duty 'rocket screens,' was crawling with rioters. They were also bombarding the station and its security cameras with paint bombs.

The New Barnsley officers, those who were on duty inside the station complex that morning, were doing all they could to maintain the integrity of their station. In the face of this onslaught, their single means of defence was plastic bullets, which of course they could only fire at those rioters who they could see. However, with little or no ambient light, it was almost impossible for them to see and identify their targets. Faced with this outrageous situation, they had quite unbelievably taken to launching flares from inside the station compound, which at least temporarily helped light up the immediate area. This enabled them to see and target those rioters, who were sitting on top of the perimeter walls and were launching wave after wave of petrol bombs into the station yard.

To help put our patrol crew's immediate situation in context, I should mention that as a consequence of the Chief Constable's initial decision, which was to ban the Drumcree parade, there had been street disorder in loyalist areas of a level the like of which hadn't been seen for many-a-long year. Due to this almost unprecedented level of disturbance, our crews had actually been deployed outside our own area, to assist the local police in controlling those riots. In those predominantly loyalist areas, where it was most unlikely that we would have been the target for terrorist gunmen, we were able to take on the rioters in an effective manner by deploying on foot, before advancing behind a shield line.

However, as we were now back in our own area, none of us needed reminding that putting our colleagues out on foot behind nothing more than a riot shield, in what was a highly volatile and extremely dangerous republican area, was an altogether different scenario.

With the majority of our crews' personnel remaining inside the vehicles, we chose to deploy two members, each armed with a Heckler & Koch 33 rifle with night site mounts, one on either side of the formation. A very brief 'confab' at the rear of the vehicles, between our patrol Sergeants and Inspector just confirmed what we had probably all already decided, we most certainly wouldn't be asking any of our men to go out on foot in this particular instance.

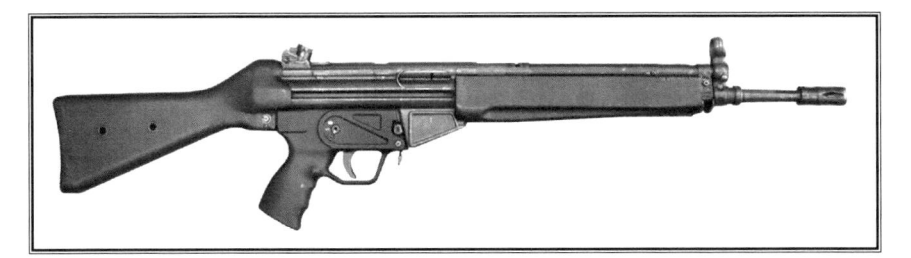

Heckler & Koch 33

Just as we were going back to our respective Land Rovers, we were suddenly totally engulfed by the noisy rattle and awesome power of incoming high-velocity gunfire! Almost instantaneously, one of the two guys who we had earlier deployed with the rifles, shouted that he had spotted the muzzle flashes of the gun which was firing at us. Returning fire at that target, he then shouted, "Watch my tracer, watch my tracer!"

Tracer rounds, for those who don't know, are bullets that are manufactured in a slightly different way from normal bullets. These tracer rounds when fired, particularly at night, are visible to the naked eye, roughly from the point it leaves the barrel of the gun until it strikes its target. Therefore, by following the line of the tracer shells which were being fired by our colleague, we could quite easily pin-down the precise location of the terrorist gunman. In all other aspects, tracer rounds are the same as normal bullets. Generally, they are loaded into the gun magazine at a ratio of around one tracer round for every four or five normal rounds.

I quickly grabbed my own rifle, another Heckler & Koch 33, which I had left sitting in the front passenger footwell of our Land Rover, and then got myself into a good safe firing position. The exchange of gunfire, between the hidden gunman and our colleague was continuing, which meant I had no problem following the track of the tracer bullets as they shot toward their intended target. Taking aim, I also returned fire, as did several others of our crew.

The follow-up operation and investigation into what had been an attempt to murder police, took place later that same morning, in the cold light of day. It revealed that the gunman had used a small alleyway in the Divismore Park area of Ballymurphy, as his firing point. That particular vantage point gave the gunman a clear and uninterrupted view of the main Springfield Road just outside New Barnsley station, and it also offered him a good level of protection. On recovering the empty shell casings from the scene, it was revealed that the terrorist had been using a rifle that fired 7.62mm ammunition and that he had fired something in the region of 40 rounds. The damaged brickwork behind and above where the gunman would have been standing bore testimony that the shots which we had fired in return, weren't too far off. In total, I discharged 17 rounds in the action.

The exchange of gunfire, which was well reported in the media, unsurprisingly had an almost immediate (& beneficial) effect on the crowds of rioters, they vanished!

CHAPTER 23

Horizontal Mortar Bomb Attack, Falls Road

Diary Date:	February 26, 1997
Incident:	Attempted Murder RUC and Army Falls Road.
Background:	Failed Mortar Bomb Attack.
Storyteller:	Gareth.

On the morning of Wednesday February 26, 1997, I was the Sergeant in charge of a four-vehicle security force patrol, (2 RUC & 2 Army) operating in West Belfast. Just before 10 a.m., whilst travelling countrywards on the Falls Road, we received a radio message instructing us to call into Andersonstown station at our earliest possible convenience. We continued our routine patrol which took us up past the Whiterock Road and the City Cemetery on our right, before passing Milltown Cemetery on our left. We then drove into the station, which was on our right immediately after the small roundabout which is at the junction of the Falls, Andersonstown and Glen Road. Whilst in the station, we were informed that the area from the station down the Falls Road as far as its junction with the Whiterock Road, had just been placed as double O.B., Out of Bounds for all security force patrols. At that time, we were given no further details as to the reason behind this directive. Consequently, we returned to our area via an alternative route.

Later that same day, at 2:38 p.m., a caller using a recognised codeword, called the offices of Ulster Television to inform them that, "Belfast brigade IRA personnel had placed a device on the Falls Road near Andersonstown barracks next to the place that makes gravestones. Our personnel placed the device there. Police Army patrol passed at 10:00 hrs today and the device failed." A second telephone call stated that, "The device was on a bridge."

The aforementioned terminology is an exact duplication of the telephoned warning which was received at the offices of UTV.

Codewords

The significance and use of a recognised codeword by the 'caller,' may not be obvious to readers who didn't live through that particularly bleak era in our country's history. A pre-determined codeword was designated too and used by each of the separate terrorist groupings in Northern Ireland. These could be used for any number of reasons, not least in order to validate the authenticity of any bomb warnings, claims or denials of responsibility for certain terrorist activities. Of course, these were just a couple of examples when codewords would be used to establish the bona fides of the messenger.

With regard to the IRA, my understanding is that that particular organisation chose their own codewords, which via an accepted and trusted channel, they then passed on to the Garda authorities in Dublin. The Garda would then communicate these directly to the security forces in Northern Ireland, who would disseminate them to all those whom they deemed it appropriate.

Back to the story:

Once that coded warning had been received, certain well-practiced routines would then swing into action. In this instance, and for the safety of the general public, the whole area from Andersonstown station, down the Falls Road as far as the Whiterock Road, was then totally cordoned off to all vehicular and pedestrian traffic.

It wasn't until the hours of daylight, from around 8-9 a.m. the following morning, that the bomb disposal personnel arrived at the scene. Only then were they able to take on the challenge of locating and defusing this reported device. If indeed it was there in the first place!

During that day's clearance operation, the officer in charge communicated that they had indeed located an explosive device, in a location that was consistent to the description given in the coded warning. At 10:28 a.m., he further reported that he and his colleagues had successfully made the device safe and that the area had once again been opened to the public.

Postscript

A post-operation report by the officer in charge of that morning's clearance, revealed that the device which they had located was what was known as a Mark 16 mortar. (See below.) As reported, it was located near to the monumental masons whose premises, on the Falls Road, sit very close to the entrance of Milltown Cemetery.

The explosive device itself, which fires horizontally, was well camouflaged. It was sitting on and under bags which were further covered in foliage and undergrowth. It would have looked something like the image below.

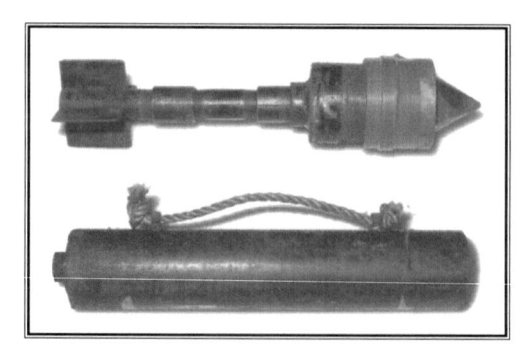

Mark 16 Mortar

The device's command wire, which was a white two-core cable, was again well-camouflaged being covered over by boulders and stones. It ran from the device through a culvert and under a small bridge, before it was embedded into the side of a small stream. The wire continued for approximately 75 metres, where it then reached the firing point in Falls Park. The terrorists did not leave behind the firing pack, which of course would have been necessary. From this well-chosen vantage point, those involved would have had a clear view of the location on the Falls Road where the device had been placed.

> "In January 1997, IRA attacks were stepped up into what became the most unsuccessful period of its entire campaign as attacks were foiled, bombs were disarmed, rockets and mortars missed their targets, and several Volunteers were captured. Such was the degree of military inefficiency that many observers began to believe that the IRA was engaged in a phoney war."[9]

As can be seen in the above cutting from de Baroid's book, this attempted mortar attack on the joint police/army patrol on February 26, wasn't the only unsuccessful attempt at murder that occurred around that time. As he mentions, despite stepping up the level of attacks it seemed that the IRA had somehow fallen into, 'the most unsuccessful period of its entire campaign as attacks were foiled, bombs were disarmed, rockets

---

9   Page 385 Ballymurphy and The Irish War. Ciarán de Baróid. First Published 1991, Reissued 2000.

and mortars missed their targets, and several volunteers were captured.' He continues this narrative by reporting that, 'Such was the degree of military inefficiency that many observers began to believe that the IRA was engaged in a phoney war.'

De Baroids inference that the reason behind so many failed operations was due to the fact 'that the IRA was engaged in a phoney war,' is of course feasible. However, an alternative hypothesis whilst much less palatable to anyone harbouring a republican psyche, may offer a more plausible explanation than the 'phoney war' premise. The well documented and accepted truth that by the mid-to-late 1990s, the republican movement was riddled with high level informers, who each reported such activities to their security force 'handlers,' would of course offer an alternative reason as to why so many of the organisation's planned operations were going wrong.

Given that the area had been designated as double O B, to the security forces some four hours before the coded warning from the terrorists was received, would undoubtedly indicate that at least some level of information had been passed onto the police beforehand.

STATEMENT

The final three stories do not relate directly to incidents involving the Bravo Delta Eight Zero patrol vehicle. But, by their inclusion, I hope the reader will be able to experience a more complete picture of what life was like for those of us who either manned that patrol vehicle or were stationed in Springfield Road station around that time.

CHAPTER 24

Attempt to Target Off-Duty Member

Diary Date:	Late 1979
Incident:	Attempt to Target Off Duty Police Officer.
Background:	Travelling Home from Night Shift.
Storyteller:	Andrew.

Background

The security threat to operational police officers across Northern Ireland was unremitting, and it most certainly didn't end when they finished their daily shifts. To illustrate the reality of this ongoing threat, here is an account of an incident that occurred to one of the crew of Bravo Delta Eight Zero, just after they had 'clocked off' from a night shift turn of duty.

Incident

After finishing nightshift as the driver of the main Springfield Road mobile patrol vehicle Bravo Delta Eight Zero, with the rest of my crew I was only too glad to be boarding the army 'taxi,' for our lift down to Hastings Street. The practice at that time, was that Springfield Road personnel parked their private cars in Hastings Street barracks, before being transported on up to Springfield Road by the military. Then at the end of our shift, we would reverse that journey. On arriving at Hastings Street, we wasted no time debussing from the 'pig,' before getting into each of our cars. We each drove out of the station complex and made our way out onto the lower Shankill Road/Peters Hill area, via a number of small side streets. There, we would split up before heading off via the city centre and onwards to our various home addresses.

Like all serving police officers of that era, I always tried to vary my route to and from my home address, just as much as was practically possible. However, after a tiring night shift, it would generally end up with me travelling country-wards in the general direction of Bangor. Unquestionably, looking to get home just as quickly as possible, this was the path (or route) of least resistance! Whilst it was common practice back then to share lifts with colleagues who travelled from the same area, that particular morning I was travelling alone on my journey home.

Around 7:30 a.m. on the morning in question, I was driving along the Sydenham Bypass approaching the Tillysburn roundabout, when I first noticed a car with three men on board, driving behind me. Just to clarify, I don't mean directly behind me in the next car, this car was driving a few vehicles back and travelling at roughly the same speed. To be honest, my initial thought was that in all probability it was three fellow policemen, who similarly had just finished their night shift and were also now travelling home.

Consequently, whilst making a mental note of their presence, I just continued my journey as normal. With most of the traffic heading towards the city, (the opposite direction) I was enjoying a relatively clear run home. As I was passing Holywood,[10] I noticed that whilst other cars seemed to be overtaking me, this particular car just seemed to be maintaining that same distance behind me. Very consciously then, I alternated slowing my car down before then speeding up again, just

---

10 Holywood outside Belfast. Not to be confused with Hollywood with two 'L's' USA.

to see how it responded. It responded in a similar fashion, seemingly determined to keep me in front of them, and as such maintain that distance.

By the time we had reached Ballyrobert, I was fairly sure that the driver and occupants of the tailing car weren't behind me by chance. Nowadays things could have been handled very differently, but of course this was long before the modern era of mobile phones, so I had no way of asking for assistance.

As we approached the junction of the Belfast Road and Rathgael Road in Bangor, the tailing car had closed up to within the distance of one car. This enabled me to get the car's registration mark, and whilst unable to get a crystal-clear look at its driver or its occupants, I could see that their general appearance was unshaven with long hair, so most unlikely to be off-duty police.

Having completed that right hand turn off the main Belfast Road and onto the Rathgael Road, I had moved from a dual carriageway onto what in essence was a small, winding country road. The suspicious car, due to being caught behind another vehicle, was still on the main carriageway and at that point hadn't been able to follow me onto the Rathgael Road. By accelerating sharply away from the junction, I was able to create a sizeable distance between our cars. Consequently, when I made the left-hand turn off Rathgael Road and onto the top of the Clandeboye Road, the tailing car wasn't in sight, so they couldn't have seen me make that turn.

I continued to drive as quickly as I could, entering deep into the labyrinth of streets that is the Kilcooley estate. I tried to double back and find a suitable position within the estate where I could park up unseen, yet still have a view of the main Clandeboye Road. I remained there for around 10-15 minutes, watching to see if the tailing car would reappear. Having waited for what seemed a reasonable amount of time and with the suspicious car not reappearing, I judged that I had indeed managed to lose it. Feeling confident enough to venture back out onto the main road, I then headed into the town centre, (closer to Bangor police station) before I took the time to drive around a bit to ensure there was nothing or no one tailing me. Eventually, I felt reassured enough to make my way home, where after reporting the incident to my station, I headed off to bed.

After a day's rest, I was then up and back into work for my next night shift. On arriving at Springfield Road and before parading for duty, my section Inspector called me down to his office to talk over that morning's incident. After hearing my account of what had happened, he went on to explain to me the details of another incident which had occurred at precisely the same time and location.

It seems that the suspicious car which had been following me, same make, model and registration, had also caught the attention of a Traffic Branch patrol vehicle which had been working in the Bangor area that morning. After carrying out a radio check on the car's registration, which had proven to be a set of 'ringer' plates, they tried to stop it. However, by hook or by crook, the suspect vehicle had somehow managed to totally evade the police Vehicle Check Point (VCP) and was last seen heading towards Belfast.

Whilst far from an ideal ending to this particular episode, it was strangely reassuring to have 100% confirmation that I hadn't been imagining things. Such was the level of threat against off-duty officers back then, that there were undoubtedly times when we perhaps became hypersensitive or even paranoid to the danger.

Postscript

As was the operational procedure regarding this sort of situation, within a few days I was issued with a set of 'security plates,' (alternate number plates which weren't registered to my home address) for my car. A case of no expense spared regarding a member's security.

CHAPTER 25

City Centre Ambush of Gerry Adams.

Diary Date:	March 14, 1984
Incident:	Attempt to Murder Gerry Adams.
Background:	Court Appearance.
Storyteller:	Samuel.

Background

On the afternoon of Wednesday March 14, 1984, an assassination attempt occurred in Belfast City Centre. Whilst hardly an earth-shattering or startling piece of news at that time in our country's arduous history, what did make this particular occurrence so newsworthy was the identity of the individual who had been targeted. West Belfast MP and recently appointed president of Sinn Fein, Gerry Adams had been attending Belfast Magistrates Court, where he and three other party members were answering charges of obstruction from an incident which had occurred the previous year. It was whilst that court was in a short recess for lunch, that he and his associates became the target of the murder attempt by the outlawed loyalist paramilitary force, the Ulster Freedom Fighters.[11]

---

11 The military wing of the Ulster Defence Association.

Unsurprisingly given the status which Gerry Adams then held in Northern Ireland and its political landscape, the newspapers of the day were saturated with reports regarding this story. However, having read through many of those contemporary newspaper articles, I believe that the most exhaustive description and undoubtedly the most nonpartisan account of that day's events, are to be found in what was a Statutory Report by the Police Ombudsman for Northern Ireland.

Some twenty-plus years after the City Centre shooting and following alleged claims which appeared in several local newspapers, that there had been some level of collusion between the security forces and the loyalist paramilitaries who had carried out the attack, Gerry Adams lodged a complaint against the police in December of 2006. Eventually, after a further seven years, on September 12, 2013, this complaint found its way to the desk of the Police Ombudsman for Northern Ireland.

Bearing in mind that the Ombudsman's office didn't open its doors until November 6, 2000, it's somewhat surprising that they would have had any authority or role in this particular matter. However, their remit, which in essence is to investigate any complaints made against police officers which are no more than 12 months old, also permits that office to 'consider matters from much longer ago, if it believes them to be grave or exceptional.' Hence their involvement in this historic investigation.

Amazingly then, over 30 years after the date of the initial shooting, in June 2014, the Ombudsman released his Statutory Report regarding this incident. The report contained a fairly detailed account of just how the events of that day had panned out, as well as publishing the conclusions of that office's investigation.

His determination concluded that.

1. There was no evidence of criminality or misconduct by any police officer, and

2. That the allegations made by Mr Adams and others had not been substantiated.

The Ombudsman's account of how that day's shooting transpired, was to a greater or lesser extent, as follows.

Gerry Adams and three co-defendants appeared in Belfast Magistrates Court on March 13, 1984, where they contested obstruction charges. These charges had arisen from an incident in the New Lodge area of Belfast, back in June of the previous year. The case ran over into a second day, which took place on Wednesday, March 14.

Shortly after 1 p.m. on that second day, the court was called into recess to allow a short break in the proceedings for lunch. Having had a request to remain within the courthouse rejected, the defendants eventually made their way out of the building, where at 1:20 p.m., they were picked up by a colleague who was driving a gold-coloured Ford Cortina car. There was nothing sinister or underhand in the courts' refusal to allow the defendants to remain within the courtroom over the lunch period. The reason was simply due to having no policy or personnel to cater for this eventuality, but the common practice back then was as it is now, to clear the courtroom.

On leaving the front of Chichester Street Court, the intention had been to drive to West Belfast, where they would have some lunch. Travelling via Oxford Street and then turning right into May Street, before continuing past the back of the City Hall and into Howard Street, the vehicle was then brought to a standstill due to heavy traffic just short of Great Victoria Street/Fisherwick Place.

A brown Rover 2000 car with three men on board, then pulled up alongside the now stationary Ford Cortina. Without warning, the three men inside the Rover, who were each armed with handguns, opened fire on the five men in the Ford Cortina.

All but one of the five people who were inside the Cortina sustained gunshot wounds, (the one person who escaped unscathed, had been sitting in the middle rear seat between two others.) The driver, despite having sustained gunshot wounds, was able to navigate a route away from the scene. He quickly made his way to the casualty department of the nearby RVH, where all those who had been injured in the attack, received immediate medical treatment.

Having raced away from the immediate scene of the ambush, the three escaping gunmen again found themselves caught up in heavy lunchtime traffic in Wellington Place. Traffic was almost at a standstill, ensuring that at this point the getaway car was well and truly 'boxed-in,' and unable to move.

Unbeknownst to the gunmen, their initial ambush had been witnessed by an off-duty soldier, who by pure coincidence had been travelling just a few cars behind them. Having seen the escaping car turn right onto Great Victoria Street, he, by cutting through Upper Queen Street and going against the one-way system, was able to intercept them as they tried to escape down Wellington Place.

Showing great courage and despite being relatively lightly armed, (he only had his personal protection weapon) and with little regard for his own safety, the soldier approached the now static car and confronted the three gunmen.

Eventually, and having been joined at the scene by other off-duty members of the security forces, the three gunmen within the car were arrested. One of whom it's reported, had sustained a 'friendly fire' gunshot wound in the ambush!

At 5:30 p.m. on the day of the shooting, a coded message was received by the BBC. The outlawed Ulster Freedom Fighters claimed responsibility for the attack, addressing Gerry Adams as being, "the Chief of Staff of the IRA, responsible for the campaign of murder and therefore a legitimate target of war."

Incident

On the morning of Wednesday 14th March 1984, along with another colleague, we 'made-up' the vehicle crew of what was back then known as the Springfield Road 'Shuttle.' Unsurprisingly given the nickname which that vehicle carried, it's role was simply to transport members from outlying locations such as Grosvenor Road or Springfield Parade, into and out of what was the much more dangerous Springfield Road barracks. Unusually, the vehicle which was routinely used for this particular role was not a Hotspur, but instead an armour plated Shorland was the vehicle of choice. Worth mentioning at this point, is that this call-sign (vehicle) would not routinely have been used to answer calls or perform normal patrols. This was mainly due to the fact that it rarely had more than two members in the vehicle crew.

That day, as was generally the case when given this particular tasking, had been quite uneventful. The early part of our shift had been very routine, transporting various police personnel back and forth, to numerous different locations throughout the Sub-Division.

At around 1:30 p.m., whilst travelling citywards on the Grosvenor Road and just having passed through the traffic lights at the Springfield/Falls/Grosvenor Road junction, we were made aware via our 'B' Division radio controller, that there had just been a shooting incident in the city centre. He further broadcast that, early reports suggested that a bronze-coloured Ford Cortina car had been badly 'shot-up,' and that it had been seen travelling country-wards on the Grosvenor Road possibly heading towards the Royal Victoria Hospital.

At this point we were literally about 50 metres or so short of the Grosvenor Road entrance to the RVH, which was on our right. I drove directly into the Royal grounds and made our way towards the little underpass area, where the RVH Casualty Department was at that time located. On rounding the tight bend which takes you to the 'drop-off' point for ambulances, we came across a bronze-coloured Ford Cortina car. It was parked up with no one onboard, just at the double entrance doors which lead directly into the casualty department. As per the radio broadcast, this car had indeed been badly shot up! It had several clusters of bullet holes and most of the windows were shattered.

As I got out of our vehicle, I was immediately approached by a man in an ambulance uniform. I have always thought this to have been somewhat bizarre, as there was absolutely no sign of any ambulances, and of course those injured in the incident had arrived there in the Cortina! Rather excitedly, he pointed to the two big black rubber doors of the casualty department, before shouting, 'They're in there, they're in there!'

The security situation back then dictated that we were unable to leave our vehicle unattended, meaning at least one of us would have to remain with the vehicle. Consequently, as I was going to be going into the hospital by myself and having absolutely no idea just what I was walking into, I withdrew my Ruger revolver from its holster, before edging my way through the double doorway. Once inside, I noticed there were lots of people seemingly scurrying about in what appeared to be a fairly wide corridor area. Medical staff were entering and exiting the trauma room, which was on your left just as soon as you came through the main doors. To try to ascertain just what was happening I made my way inside. There were numerous casualties, from memory two or three, lying on beds and being attended to by doctors and nurses.

There seemed to be blood everywhere, however I did notice that one of the casualties seemed to have sustained particularly severe wounds to his face. I didn't at that time recognise any of those who were in that area.

After a short time a member of the nursing staff ushered me out of the trauma room, and back out to the corridor area. By this stage I was shocked to find there was even more people hanging about in that area of the hospital, including several really well-known Republicans.

I noticed that one of those in this group of people was a man with longish hair and a beard. Like those in the trauma unit, he seemed to be saturated in blood. As I approached and I'm nearly sure it was before I had even spoken a word to him, he very aggressively addressed me. Perhaps not using these precise words he said, "My name is such and such, my address is such and such, and my date of birth is such and such!" To finish he made it abundantly clear that he would be saying nothing else to me and that I could "**** off!" I was later to learn that this man was actually the one person out of the five in the Cortina, who hadn't actually been hit by any of the gunfire of the would-be loyalist assassins.

At the time it seemed to me that I had been inside the Casualty Department alone for ages, but in all probability, it really wasn't that long. I was however so pleased when I was eventually joined in the hospital by additional police officers. I seem to remember it was actually two vehicle crews from our neighbouring Andersonstown station, who were the first to arrive. I eventually got access to a telephone, enabling me to ring our radio control room to report on just what was happening.

Then, as the Andersonstown Sergeant and I were standing at the door of the Trauma room, one of the prominent republicans who had seemingly just appeared from nowhere, emerged from the trauma room and proceeded to run away up the corridor, before we saw him dart into a side office. Accompanied by the Sergeant, we immediately pursued him as we tried to ascertain just what he was up to. Somehow or other by the time we had reached the door of the office, he had managed to block it from the inside. However, after a bit of pushing and shoving, which ensured we each had an up close and personal encounter with this well-known figure, we eventually did manage to force our way in. We were only able to have a very cursory look around, but before we could commence a detailed search of the office, a member of the nursing staff appeared and insisted that we all leave the office.

Very shortly after this particular occurrence, my colleague and I were relieved from our duty at the Royal, allowing us to return to the much more mundane role of 'shuttling' colleagues back and forth.

Postscript

In the course of their investigation at the scene of the actual shooting, the police located twelve empty cartridge cases. In Wellington Place where the three arrests occurred, three handguns and seven live rounds were recovered.

On examination of the target car, which had been located and subsequently recovered from the casualty department of the RVH, they noted it had been struck nine times. No shots had been discharged by any members of the security forces. The police investigation further revealed that it had been the gunmen's original intention to have mounted their attack the previous day. However, as that plan didn't work out, they returned on the second day of the accused's court case.

In March of the following year 1985, three loyalists were convicted and received long custodial sentences, for their part in this shooting.

Another thought-provoking aspect of this particular story relates to Tom Travers, the Resident Magistrate who had presided over the initial court case involving Gerry Adams and his three co-accused. On the day of the shooting, quite understandably Mr Travers adjourned the case, rescheduling it to be heard on April 12. However, by a most cruel twist of fate, just four days before that date, the IRA attempted to assassinate Tom Travers.

On that Sunday morning of April 8, just as Mr Travers and two of his family, his wife Joan and daughter Mary, were leaving St. Brigit's Roman Catholic Church in South Belfast, two masked gunmen ambushed the small family group. Despite being hit by six bullets, all fired from point blank range, thankfully Mr Travers manage to survive the attack. His wife Joan also had what can only be described as an extraordinary escape! It's reported that one of the gunmen deliberately took aim and pointed his weapon at Mrs Travers head, before pulling the guns trigger twice! Miraculously on each occasion, the gun misfired! Mrs Travers escaped the attack with no physical injuries!

However, his daughter Mary, who was only 22 years old at the time, wasn't so fortunate. She was hit in the spine area by a single bullet, tragically she lost her life in that day's attack.

Mr Travers surviving daughter Ann, who for many years has been a brave campaigner for victim's rights, records that after the shooting of her father, the case against Gerry Adams and his three co-accused was dismissed and that it has never been reheard.

CHAPTER 26

No Creed in Duty
Paratrooper Sgt. Michael Willets

Diary Date:	May 25, 1971
Incident:	Murder of Paratroop Sergeant Michael Willets.
Background:	Bomb Attack on Springfield Road.
Storyteller:	Andrew.

Introduction

As I tried to bring this work to a close, I confess that I found myself caught up in a bit of a quandary! This related to something which had been eating-away at me since I started the project, and in all honesty, persisted through just about every single conversation I had with ex-colleagues whilst carrying out my research.

From the outset, and indeed from even a quick glance at the front cover, this memoir very deliberately focuses on what life was like for RUC officers in Springfield Road mobile patrols. However, and I'm guessing you knew that word was coming! However, the more I pondered this issue, the more convinced I became that any written work relating to Springfield Road RUC station, which didn't include a respectful reference to this particular story, would be work that was incomplete and perhaps even inappropriate!

I'm referring of course to the tragic story of British Army Paratrooper, Sergeant Michael Willets who lost his life whilst trying to save members of the public, inside Springfield Road RUC station. As we all now know, regrettably Sergeant Willets wasn't the only member of the security forces to lose their life in and around the station premises. Of course, there is absolutely no sleight meant or implied to those who I haven't mentioned. This was never meant to be an exhaustive or all-inclusive piece of work.

So, here it is, my retelling of it.

"Another bloody chapter in an endless civil war!"

Background

The British Army, at the behest of the UK Government, arrived in Northern Ireland as a peacekeeping force in August of 1969. The province was seemingly on the verge of a bloody civil war, as the vastly undermanned police force of the day, struggled to maintain any semblance of law and order in the face of widespread sectarian unrest.

The expressed fear of the British authorities had always been that whilst it would be a relatively easy task to deploy the army in the province, actually getting them back out again would prove to be much more difficult!

That deployment, which was given the operational name of 'Op Banner,' proved just how well-founded that fearful thinking was. Quite unbelievably, it would be almost thirty-eight years later that the Op Banner deployment would eventually be brought to an end. As such, it is now acknowledged as being the longest continual deployment of military personnel in the history of the British Army.

On the ground in 1969, after experiencing an all too brief honeymoon period which initially saw the Army welcomed by members of the Roman Catholic community, it wasn't long before that relationship had become much more acrimonious! By the early 1970s, the neighbourhood deployments of army regiments had gone from being the defender and champion of the local communities, to being considered the enemy and the target of murderous attacks by the IRA.

The Army's first fatality occurred on February 6, 1971, when 20-year-old Robert Curtis of the Royal Artillery Regiment, was shot whilst on public order duty in the New Lodge area of North Belfast. Sergeant Willets, who was the army's eighth fatality of Op Banner, was killed just three months later in the same year. This is his story.

Incident

At around 8:24 p.m. on Tuesday May 25, 1971, a civilian car pulled to a stop just outside Springfield Road RUC Station. From the front passenger seat an unknown young male emerged and made his way in through the front doors of the barracks. As he entered the station hallway, he was carrying a small brown suitcase which had a smoking fuse protruding from it. Once inside, he quickly dumped the case and fled back out of the station, into the waiting car before speeding away.

The exact sequence of the happenings which took place in those last few seconds before the bomb exploded, appear to have got somewhat jumbled-up. After a thorough read through the many contemporary newspapers, undoubtedly there are some minor inconsistencies to be found in their reporting of this story. Such minor variations in the retelling of any story are of course quite normal, as each person's perception of any incident, never mind one as shocking as this one, can be somewhat different. However, there is one very clear and consistent narrative which runs throughout each of the testimonies, and it relates to the heroic part played by Paratrooper Sergeant Michael Willets.

Just before the terrorist had entered the front doors and thrown the bomb into the open public area of the station enquiry office, two local police officers, a Detective Sergeant and a Detective Constable had been walking through the hallway and going towards those doors. They had momentarily paused to have a chat with two small children who were already in the enquiry office with their parents. The Detective Constable is later quoted as saying that he and his Sergeant, "Were talking to the people when the suitcase landed only a few feet away from us. We knew what it must be and helped hustle them out of the way. We had about ten seconds and then it went off."

When the terrorist placed the smoking suitcase bomb onto the floor of the station enquiry office, it seems that Sergeant Willets wasn't actually in that immediate area. However, on hearing the Detective Sergeant who was the first to raise the alarm, shouting, "Get out of the way, there's a bomb!" Sergeant Willets, showing little or no thought for his own personal safety, immediately dashed to the scene to see how he could help. On his arrival, he caught sight of the smoking device which was sitting on the floor in the hall!

Shouting clear instructions to all his staff who were within earshot, he told them to evacuate the building. At the same time, and to help the police officers clear the immediate area beside the bomb, Sergeant Willets quickly opened an adjoining door that led out of the hall and into an adjacent corridor. Taking up a standing position in the doorway to keep the door open, he remained there, physically ushering the police officers and the members of the public out past him and into the corridor. He maintained that position until he was absolutely sure that the hallway containing the bomb, had been completely evacuated, barring himself!

In the scramble to escape the immediate area of the bomb, it appears that some sort of obstruction occurred in the adjoining corridor, temporarily hindering those who were using it as a getaway. The last in the line of 'escapees' who were ushered to safety by Sergeant Willets, was an RUC Inspector. He, then effectively became a shield to those in front of him.

Regrettably, it appears that just as Sergeant Willets had ushered the Inspector out of immediate danger, and before he could himself move to a safer location, the bomb exploded! As a consequence, he took the full force of the explosion, suffering catastrophic head injuries.

Those who he had just directed out of the hall and into the side corridor, thankfully avoided the worst of the explosion, by a split second! The RUC Inspector, who at the time of the explosion was in the position of being tail-end-Charlie in that small line of 'escapees,' was blown off his feet! Miraculously though, he ended up lying flat out over the top of the two children, shielding them as heavy debris, rubble and shards of glass cascaded all around them. Somehow or other, they each suffered little more than superficial injuries.

The force of the explosion not only blew inwards and towards the barracks as had been the intention of the attack, of course, it also blew upwards and outwards across the main Springfield Road. Unfortunately, just at that time a local mother was pushing her two-year-old baby boy in his pram, down the road on the opposite footpath. Both were caught up in the explosion, with the baby ultimately being diagnosed as having suffered a fractured skull in the bomb attack. Whilst the mother was patched up and released from hospital the following day, the baby wasn't so fortunate, going on to spend the next two months of his young life as an inpatient at the hospital.

By a strange quirk of fate, it was the injured baby's 14-year-old elder brother who actually pulled the baby out of the rubble, before carrying his young sibling down to the Royal Victoria Hospital. He had just chanced upon the scene of the bomb, after hearing the explosion and walking round to the scene from his nearby home address.

Press reports at the time, speculated that there had been between 20 – 30lbs of gelignite in the Springfield Road bomb. Whether that estimate was correct or not, the explosion absolutely devastated the immediate area around the station hallway and front office.

Twenty-six people (civilians and members of the security forces alike) suffered injuries in this no-warning attack. But considering the size of the bomb and the absolute recklessness shown by the terrorists who planted it, the injuries were comparatively light. Unquestionably this was in no small part due to the bravery and totally selfless actions of Sergeant Willets, who that day went well above and beyond what could reasonably have been expected of him. To ensure others were safe, he took the brunt of the brutal explosion.

Despite suffering horrendous injuries, he bravely hung on to life as his broken body was dug out of the debris. Whilst resting on the remains of a wooden door, he was then carried clear of the wreckage before being placed in one of the fleet of ambulances which had by then rushed to the scene. In their coverage of this incident, the newspapers do mention that just as the casualty was being carried out of the debris, a crowd of local republican youths noisily jeered those who were attending to the needs of the dying and the injured! Sadly, Sergeant Willets succumbed to the horrific injuries he had sustained some two hours later, whilst in the operating theatre of the nearby Royal Victoria Hospital.

The two civilians, neighbours, who had been in the station at the time of the bomb, had gone to the RUC Station together to speak to local police regarding a parking issue. They were both fulsome in their praise of all those who had played a part in keeping them safe, particularly so of Sergeant Willets.

Mrs Cummings, who was accompanied by her young son Carl, said, "In the middle of all the confusion, the Sergeant was a centre of absolute calm. Such courage cannot be compared to the actions of men who throw bombs among innocent people."

Her neighbour, Mr Grey, reflected that whilst in the station enquiry office, a young man had suddenly burst in through the front doors and hurled a suitcase across the floor of the hallway. He went on to say, "I didn't know where the hell to run when the bomb landed. I grabbed the kids by the scruff of the neck-and there was this soldier standing braced by the door to show us where to go. But for him we would have been dead, he was the last person in the room, standing there making sure we were all safe. There was a split second of complete silence, then it went off. The Sergeant took the full blast…"

At 8.45 a.m. on Friday, May 28, Paratrooper Sergeant Michael Willets' Union Jack draped coffin was being carried on an open gun carriage, as part of a column of military vehicles on the Springfield Road. The vehicles were making their way towards the station, where they would be met by around 200 of his ex-colleagues and over 100 RUC men. Standing to attention, they solemnly waited the arrival of the fallen soldier, as a final and ultimate mark of respect.

Coming less than 72 hours after the bomb-blast which had brought death and destruction to the very heart of this local police station, undoubtedly the building was looking rather unkempt. But with a bugle corp now standing out proudly on the buildings flat roof, and the Parachute Regiments flag still flying over the station, (albeit at that time half-mast) the subliminal message really couldn't have been any clearer.

Yes, we may be battered and bruised! Hurting? Absolutely! But beaten? Never!

On its arrival outside the station, the procession came to a stop. As the buglers, from their elevated rooftop position, sounded the 'Last Post' and during the succeeding one minutes silence, there was barely a sound to be heard! The Regiments flag was then raised back to full mast, as the buglers sounded 'Reveille.' A small crowd of locals had gathered to witness what was a very moving few moments, before after taking a salute from the Regiments Commanding Officer, the cortège moved off again. It then continued its journey to Aldergrove Airport, from whence Sergeant Willets body would be repatriated home to Nottinghamshire, where a small personal funeral would take place the following Tuesday.

Sergeant Michael Willets funeral.
Belfast Telegraph Friday May 28, 1971..

Postscript

Whilst the finer details of this tragic story would be unknown to most, I'm guessing that the broad tale of Sergeant Willets may seem oddly familiar to many of us of a certain age. That familiarity probably stems from the fact that his story was put to music and released as a single record back in the early 1970s.

It never got airtime on any of the BBC radio channels at the time, as the Corporation deemed it may be offensive to the nationalist population in Northern Ireland, and therefore banned its broadcasting. Despite this very deliberate attempt to veto the record and the significant difficulties in obtaining a copy, one record shop on the loyalist Shankill Road reported that they alone had sold 5,000 copies.

Whether pirate copies or genuine records, many '45s' did make their way onto the record players of homes in Northern Ireland. Unsurprisingly it also became a greatly loved folksong in the pubs and clubs of loyalist areas throughout the province.

Epilogue

It is not the critic who counts
Nor the man who points out how
the strong man stumbles
Or the doer of the deeds
could have done better.
The credit belongs to the man
who is actually in the arena;
whose face is marred by dust
and sweat and blood;
Who knows great enthusiasm,
great devotion and the triumph
of achievement.
And who, at the worst, if he fails
at least fails whilst daring greatly
so that his place shall never be
with those odd and timid souls
who know neither victory nor defeat.
You've never lived until you've almost died.
For those who have had to fight for it
Life has truly a flavour
the protected shall never know

Theodore Roosevelt's well-known quote regarding striving valiantly and daring greatly, written in 1910, could easily have been written for and about the Royal Ulster Constabulary (RUC).

Contemporary data protection regulations are now so rigid that they make gaining access to official information and records of occurrences involving the police, even regarding incidents that occurred more than 40 years ago, an impossible task. Essentially then, each individual testimony you have read came about as a result of one officer knowing other officers from Springfield Road RUC Station.

We do not doubt that if the officer who helped structure these stories had been given access to the files and records from that era, even in a restricted or supervised fashion, it would have been possible to have written not one book but a complete library of them. We're sure many of his ex-colleagues will be saying to themselves, "You've forgotten that incident," or "flip, remember the night such and such happened!"

It really is unfortunate that so many stories of service, stories of courage and acts of simple human kindness by so many very brave public servants, could be lost forever in the sands of time. The only way of saving them is for each of us to tell our stories, so the generations to come will have the truth.

About the Author

Whilst this book is indeed a collection of true stories from numerous RUC officers, the stories have been collated, written and published by just one person, the author, Andrew.

Since what was undoubtedly a hazardous 3-year initiation to his service within the RUC at Springfield Road, he went on to serve the remainder of his 25-year career in different stations and departments.

Having been brought up in what was a typical Northern Ireland working class Presbyterian Church background, and consequently been well schooled in the spiritual aims of the Boys Brigade movement, The Advancement of Christ's Kingdom Among Boys, he eventually came to a personal, living faith in Christ many years later.

The circumstances of his conversion were that whilst serving in East Belfast's Strandtown station, remarkably he found that his specific police section was disproportionately numbered with Christian colleagues. Those colleagues lived out their Christian faith in front of him on a daily basis and their testimonies and lifestyles left a lasting impression on him. Unquestionably under conviction during that period of his life, circumstances would however see him move on and transfer away from that particularly influential environment.

Besides taking him away from what was undoubtedly a strong Christian influence on his life, that career move also saw him more exposed than ever to some of the most dangerous elements of policing which occurred throughout the Northern Ireland troubles.

Then, by a most strange set of circumstances, one of those Christian colleagues with whom he had served in Strandtown station came back into his life. It was the renewal of this relationship and after many long and deep conversations, that he ultimately came to Christian faith.

Now safely into retirement, he and his wife spend their time together, enjoying life with their extended family and friends. They are very grateful to God for his hand upon both their lives, bringing them through what was a very difficult period.

Reflecting on those times with former comrades over the past 45 years, there is now a deeper awareness of the gravity of the situations they faced back then. Despite suffering lifelong mental health challenges from his service, the author's sentiment remains clear: given the same circumstances, the choice would be the same—I would do it all over again.

To contact the author

Send an email to:

author@MauriceWylieMedia.com

Place in subject bar: Andrew Martin

Inspired To Write A Book?

Contact

Maurice Wylie Media
Your Inspirational & Christian Book Publisher

Based in Northern Ireland and distributing around the world.

www.MauriceWylieMedia.com